Healthy Disclosure

Healthy Disclosure

Solving Communication Quandaries in Congregations

Kibbie Simmons Ruth and Karen A. McClintock

THE
ALBAN
INSTITUTE
Herndon, Virginia
www.alban.org

The Alban Institute
2121 Cooperative Way, Suite 100
Herndon, VA 20171

Scripture quotations, unless otherwise noted, are from the New Revised Standard Version of the Bible, © 1989, Division of Christian Education of the National Council of Churches of Christ in the United States of America, and are used by permission.

Cover design by Adele Robey, Phoenix Graphics.

Library of Congress Cataloging-in-Publication Data

Ruth, Kibbie Simmons
  Healthy disclosure : solving communication quandaries in congregations / Kibbie Simmons Ruth and Karen A. McClintock.
      p. cm.
  Includes bibliographical references.
  ISBN 978-1-56699-346-3
  1. Communication—Religious aspects—Christianity. I. McClintock, Karen A., 1953- II. Title.

  BV4597.53.C64R88 2007
  253—dc22
                                        2007023552

  11   10   09   08   07   UG   1   2   3   4   5

Contents

Foreword

Since the later part of the 1970s there has been a growing literature (and concern) about secrets in families, churches, synagogues, and the workplace. Now our everyday conversation is peppered with "elephants in the room," "triangles," and "dysfunction" (usually related to "don't talk" rules). I, for one, have found a good deal of the insights related to the concepts behind this jargon to be helpful, thought provoking, and producing levels of understanding of organizational behavior that were confusing to me.

But a good deal of what was out there about secrets was also confounding. Sometimes I felt that those who were developing these new theories about systems and families were telling me that secrets were always toxic, and I wasn't allowed to have any. I felt it was being recommended that after a particularly grizzly, horrific, or salacious occurrence that consultants should help people go through a cathartic investigation/revelation that would wipe the slate clean so all could begin new and cleansed, if no longer innocent. I don't know what your experience was, but I was not renewed by Ken Starr's revelations of Bill Clinton's abusive behavior with a White House intern. In that case the public had more revealed to it than was necessary, not at all increasing my trust in government and its processes or satisfying me that justice was being done.

Secrets, respect for privacy, confidentiality, it seems to me, have a place in my life and in the lives of other individuals and in organizations. Sometimes I feel that an aggressive systems consultant believes that since the confession of a penitent to a priest is salvific, it may be doubly so in front of a congregation. And what of the congregation? Does it need to know the details of the confession, or even that it occurred? On occasion it does, but it may not need to know all the details, and it is unlikely the larger group will be healed by hearing the details. In this commonsense, rational, well-researched, and down-to-earth book, Ruth and Mc-Clintock have taken the dreadful menace out of secrets and their disclosure (when appropriate). Here we learn there are times (and appropriate places) when certain information should not be kept secret but needs to be shared. The book helps the congregational leader explore in times of inappropriate behavior and crisis such questions as: What is meant by confidential? When should there be limited sharing with others? Who are the others that should be in on the information, and what do they need to know? When should there be broader sharing with the congregation, and what are the limits of that sharing?

When confronting these difficult situations what is so beneficial about this book is that the definitions and strategies found here are clear, in-depth, and complete. So those responsible in a congregation have clear reasons for determining what needs to be shared, who needs to know, and how to share it.

And the book goes beyond just reflecting on how to deal with improper sexual or financial behavior; the authors also explore ways to deal with information related to everyday concerns such as giving, illness, personal sharing, gossip, rumors, and others. Not all of these have to do with criminal or unethical behavior, some of the concerns here have to do with that which diminishes trust and a sense of community or could lead to disappointment and frustration in the life of a community of faith.

When dealing with improper behavior or policies concerning sharing in a congregation, churches and synagogues (especially smaller ones) tend to operate out of an ad hoc management style, especially in relation to activities that did not happen regularly in the past. Management theory and process gets made up as the group goes along. Often it is made up of an amalgam of practices learned at work, in other congregations of which the leaders were a part, or from the creativity of folks just trying to get along in the speediest, uncomplicated, and least anxiety-producing ways. Often leaders do not have time (or interest) to study the denomination's standards for management and decision making or the fairly substantial literature on healthy congregational practices. (How many times have we heard Episcopalians complaining that this church is getting to "congregational" or congregationalists worrying about the clergy being too hierarchical?) It takes a lot of energy, thinking, and time to explore what one's denominational group or researchers in management have learned over the years. In difficult situations leaders often use rule #1—"Do what will reduce or eliminate anxiety." In other words, the strategies are almost entirely palliative and do little to restore health or take preventive measures for possible future problems (the congregation's or someone else's). Sometimes these inadequate strategies also avoid following the law, which may require certain kinds of disclosure (to the state, the congregation, and sometimes the public at large). With the insights in this book, congregational leaders can get a perspective on how they can be less ad hoc and function more out of the standards of their denomination and out of better management policies.

There will be many who benefit from the insights and strategies promulgated here. Most especially those who work with congregations as consultants or denominational executives will definitely want to become expert with the definitions, analytical questions, and strategies described here. If you're a consultant to congregations, this book will definitely supply a great deal of what you need to be a sage helper related to disclosure in congregational life. The book will also be of help to clergy. It will help them think through possible difficulties related to counseling, confidentiality, and public prayer. It should be a heads-up for them reducing the chance of getting into awkward situations. And both clergy and lay leaders (especially board members and members of personnel committees) should review the material in this book to become familiar with its recommendations about organizational policy related to personnel, volunteers working with children, the sharing of member's financial information, and so forth. Finally, the book should be put in a congregation's first aid kit for removal and use if and when a bad thing happens to good people. When bad stuff happens this will be one of the most valuable resources the leadership of a congregation can have.

So, this is not just a book for dysfunctional organizations or congregations facing a crisis, it is also a helpful manual for everyday congregational management and thoughtful, faithful community development. It is realistic about what happens and what can be done in a variety of congregational settings.

Speed B. Leas

Acknowledgments

With humility and gratitude we thank our spouses for dealing well with their abandonment issues during this project. We appreciate our families for giving us laughter and breaks in the writing process. Our editor, Beth Gaede, is due many thanks for her ability to bring clarity out of our confusion and her kindness throughout the process. We also offer kudos to the two talented attorneys who reviewed the chapter on legal issues. We are grateful to Joy Melton for her work alongside ours in creating safer congregations.

We also express our thanks to the clergy and lay leaders who have provided us with inside views of congregational life. We are determined to assist others in avoiding some of the mistakes that have dearly cost congregations and individuals within them. Too many congregations have been and continue to be wounded by inappropriate disclosures and failures to disclose.

We share a passion for healthy congregations. We recognize the powerful witness of loving communities of people who help others in an isolated and a hurting world. We thank our teachers in the creation of healthy and holy sanctuaries and our forebears in this work. Working with the "hot topic" of sexuality has also taught us that too much or too little can be disclosed at any time, even by those with the best of intentions. Both of us have occasionally said too much or said too little in our ministries. By the grace of God we convict ourselves, correct ourselves, laugh a little, cry a little, and do it all again. May this grace bless all of you as well.

Introduction

The average conversation contains between 150 and 200 words per minute. Most of these words fly from our mouths with little forethought and sometimes with disastrous results. What did you say about yourself today? How much did you reveal, to whom, and why? This is a book about conscious communication, which requires intentional consideration and awareness of every information exchange.

How much is disclosed in congregations, by whom, to whom, when, where, and why? These questions keep coming up in our work as congregational consultants. Many, if not most, congregations fall into patterns of unconscious communication, leading to disastrous interpersonal and organizational outcomes. Congregational conflicts and dysfunction often involve poor information management, currently or in the past. Leaders may not realize that they do not have the necessary information to effectively govern the congregation. What information they do have may be distorted. On the other hand, sensitive or personal information may be inadvertently dispersed without regard for consequences. Making *conscious* communication decisions improves overall congregational health.

The old adage that sticks and stones break bones but words never hurt is blatantly false. A university professor explained that he spends his whole day communicating. Eighty percent of the

time he is clear, and twenty percent of the time he is busy trying
to correct a mistake or to counter a misinterpretation of what he
has said. The percentages in congregations may not be much better. This resource is designed to raise the awareness of clergy and
lay leaders about communication blunders in their congregations
so they can manage information more effectively.

Our particular concern is that congregational vitality is too often
destroyed by harmful, often unconscious communication, such as
passing on misinformation, keeping secrets, disclosing confidences,
and spreading insidious gossip and slander. Communication patterns that are indirect, reduce relational respect, or unnecessarily
expose private information can destroy a faith community. Conflicts
cannot be resolved without learning healthy disclosure. Abuses of
power will continue to plague congregations if we don't address
the unnecessary silences that make room for secrets. On the other
hand, overdisclosure by clergy and lay leaders can have similar
negative effects on the congregation.

Many factors need to be considered when determining what
constitutes appropriate disclosure. Both the content of the communication and the process by which it is handled are crucial.
For example, if a pastor tells church members in the prayer group
about his troubled marriage, his private information (his thoughts
and feelings) becomes open to public scrutiny. He is also disclosing in a broader context confidential information belonging to his
wife. However, his communication could be safe and appropriate
if he talked to the chairperson of the church's personnel committee to explain his request for more time off with his family. Yet,
if the chairperson was anxious about what the pastor told him
and passed it along to the whole committee, without his permission, the disclosure might become problematic. If the committee
members didn't have an agreement that they would limit access
to the information related to personnel and told their partners
and spouses, more people would know personal and potentially
damaging information about the pastor. If the pastor shared the
information with a newly single woman in the congregation, that

would also create problems. His vulnerable communication may appear to be needy and could be open to various interpretations. She might interpret the information as intimate sharing and the budding of a romantic relationship—or sexual harassment.

Many clergy and lay leaders are unprepared to make conscious decisions about how to deal with potentially volatile information. How do you respond to e-mail attacks sent by a parishioner as blind copies so that no one knows who else received the communication? How does a personnel committee announce a staff firing without appearing to be hiding information, while at the same time protecting privacy and avoiding public slander? In a counseling session, how does the rabbi process information received from a family member that the grandmother is being neglected or abused? What does the rabbi do about her commitment to confidentiality and her legal and ethical mandate to file a protective report? The answers to these and dozens of other disclosure dilemmas are addressed in this book.

As consultants, we are often asked to work with congregations after many communication mistakes have been made. Even in times of crisis, congregations can learn and practice new skills and conscious communication management. This book reveals what each of us has learned from many years of congregational consulting.

The first four chapters identify common disclosure mistakes in congregations. We begin chapter 1 with an exploration of how and why faith leaders tend to disclose too much or too little. What motivates healthy and unhealthy patterns of disclosure? Chapters 2 and 3 explore secrets kept by clergy and congregations and the damaging consequences of nondisclosure. But secret keeping isn't the only destructive communication process in faith communities. Too much disclosure, in the form of rumors, gossip, leaks of protected information, and exposure (telling far too much personal information), also create harmful interpersonal and organizational dynamics. Chapter 4 looks at those communication styles. These opening chapters assist clergy and lay leaders in understanding motivations, biases, and institutional realities that come into play as they make disclosure decisions. Although damaging, many of these habits can be healed, and the steps to heal them are offered later in the book.

Congregations easily get off course in their management of information, but course corrections are possible when leaders are more knowledgeable in their decision making about communication. In chapter 5 we clarify the levels of information dissemination so that congregations improve their communication in pulpit announcements, in pastoral counseling, in committee-meeting discussions, and even in specific letters to members and constituents. Chapter 6 recommends that leaders consider who has a *right* to know and who has the *need* to know certain information.

Out of fear of being sued, faith leaders too often fail to disclose information needed to protect others or needed for healthy community life. Chapter 7 is designed to assist leaders when they must assess their level of risk in making disclosures. This chapter is not legal advice, but it includes a review of legal issues related to disclosure.

Decisions require leaders to contemplate their own motivations, needs, and roles within the congregation, and they need to know their congregation's culture, values, and governance. These issues are addressed in chapter 8. A more specific decision-making process is described in chapter 9, using a case study. Chapter 10 includes practical guidance about ways to clean up nasty communication habits. Chapter 11 highlights specific areas involving complicated disclosures, such as information about predecessor clergy, donor records, information sharing among staff, and public records related to registered sex offenders. The book concludes with the scriptural mandate for appropriate disclosure, "speaking the truth in love."

In light of our work as consultants, we make several basic assumptions about disclosure and congregational health. Our first assumption is that *the more conscious we are of what we are doing* with the information we have and pass along to others, the better off our congregations will be. The use of the prayer chain to spread news of someone's prostate surgery without asking permission to do so is an example of unconscious disclosure that can and does damage individuals on a regular basis.

A second assumption is that clergy and lay leaders are *information trustees*—that is, people who are entrusted with intimate details and complicated stories from the lives of parishioners. As such, one of the first obligations in the role of congregational leaders is to act in a trustworthy manner, whether the information is about a giving record, a former staff member, or a sexual abuse incident in a parish family.

Knowledge is power is another important assumption. In congregations, as in other organizations, a person's status in the community is determined by what he or she knows. Lawyers know more than front-desk clerks. Clergy know more than Sunday school teachers. This isn't to say that they are more intelligent but simply that more people trust them and therefore give them more of the information needed to make decisions. The power to make a good decision begins by having all the relevant information. Where secrets abound and crucial information is withheld, power is distorted. The elected leaders are not able to actually lead when people who shield the old secrets possess unwarranted power in the congregation. The power of secrets and in withholding necessary information threatens individual safety and damages congregational integrity and health.

We assume that while congregations can and often do develop poor communication habits, *these learned behaviors can be unlearned*. Gossip and rumor can be eliminated. Triangulation can be stopped. In our consulting we have seen individuals within congregations shape entirely new patterns of healthy disclosure that have led to personal and organizational growth.

Congregations can achieve *transparency* in their communication. Transparency establishes trust by requiring that leaders and members have sufficient information to make wise decisions, by eliminating secrets, and by expecting that everyone tells the truth. Jesus's teaching that "the truth will make you free" (John 8:32) is relevant today. Truth-telling is advised unless certain dynamics or factors suggest otherwise. Transparency involves determining what you cannot share, then telling all you can, while explaining the limitations of the protected information.

Information management is a technical process and, even more important, a spiritual undertaking. Most of these decisions boil down to the simple question, what do we disclose? Leaders need the ability to use spiritual discernment in solving congregational dilemmas. Information must be handled in light of the potential harm and benefit to various parties and to the functioning of organizations. In our litigious culture, civil liability must be included along with faith when discerning how to use information.

God can move and work powerfully in and through congregations, particularly those that are safe places—physically, emotionally, and spiritually. Safe congregations are created when leaders take their role as information trustees seriously, act with transparency, and remain conscious in their communication.

Chapter 1

Why Do We Talk Too Much
or Talk Too Little?

Congregational leaders, both lay and clergy, are trustees of information about people's lives. The fact that Ron's surgery left him with side effects that affected his sexual performance isn't something to talk about in the pastoral prayer. But in one congregation, on the new pastor's first Sunday, a woman announced during prayer time, "If you are wondering why the last pastor moved to another church, it's because he was having an affair with me." Prayer time is one of many venues in a congregation where private information becomes public, and public information is often shared. Some of the information about individual lives within the community of the faithful needs to be concealed and other information needs to be revealed. Decisions about which is which cannot be made casually.

Like other professionals, clergy must take great care in the disclosure of personal information in congregations. When information is disclosed haphazardly, the congregation loses trust in the authority of the pastoral office as well as the individual pastor. Clergy aren't the only influential leaders in a church, however. Even when lay leaders betray the information congregants have entrusted to them (for example, telling someone the new member's pledge amount), the congregation can go into a slow and unexamined decline. When disclosures take place that wound or injure people, the very foundation of trust necessary for healthy ministries is undermined.

Worse yet, when silence is kept about dangerous situations such as a conviction of sexual abuse, people are left unprotected and the damage may be so great that it cannot always be healed.

This book is based on the understanding that clergy and pastoral leaders are "information trustees" for their congregations. Each relationship has within it the power to wound and the power to heal. When leaders are entrusted with sensitive information about matters such as spirituality, sexuality, family secrets, and shameful behaviors, they must treat the information with sensitivity and respect. What to keep private and what to disclose, what to share for the protection of others and what to pass on for the liberation of the community must be thoughtfully considered. These are the daily decisions that can create health or disease within congregations. What we say to and about each other can form the basis of loving community or it can undermine a leader's authority and erode a congregation.

How then are lay leaders and clergy accountable to the members of congregations in their job as information trustees? First, they must become exceptionally conscious of the information they are given and what they do with it. Second, they must analyze their own motivations for disclosing the information or withholding it. Third, they must clearly articulate to the congregation the information to which it has and does not have access and reasons for those differences.

Patterns of Disclosure

"Disclosure" is a process of revealing information to others. There are levels of disclosure; people who have just met each other disclose less than those who are old friends. Each disclosure we make has the power to build or to break down interpersonal relationships, including both nuclear and congregational families.

We all have learned rules about what to disclose and what to keep secret. Learned disclosure patterns affect our decisions as information trustees. When an issue comes up in a congregation, we will likely respond to it from past experience with privacy and secrecy. We all learned what could be shared and what must be private in our families and cultures of origin. We acquire rules about what to say from our culture, such as the rule that politics or religion shouldn't be discussed at a party. Some of these rules are conscious and some are more instinctual. Our emotional responses and our familial communication patterns combine to influence what we will disclose.

Patterns Learned from Family

Do you remember when you were a child and someone asked you to keep a secret? Secrets that young children frequently are asked to keep are about happy experiences. Perhaps an older sibling has an upcoming birthday and everyone is asked to keep quiet about the plans. But sometimes children learn that there are things they shouldn't tell because someone will feel uncomfortable about the disclosure. Common things that families don't talk about include someone's excessive drinking, angry outbursts, physical abuse, sexual boundary crossings, or even changes in family income. Children come to believe that talking about these problems will result in their being punished or even worse, escalate the parents' fighting, end an important relationship, or destroy the family.

Spoken and unspoken family rules teach us what to talk about and what not to talk about. Each family has its own communication patterns. Within those patterns, some families are open about family dynamics, sexuality, and other relationships issues. Other families may learn to protect themselves and others by saying very little, especially about "touchy" subjects. Depending on cultural background, we may choose a level of disclosure based on our desire to honor our family and ancestral heritage.

As we become old enough to conform or to rebel (or some combination of both), we make choices about what to say, to whom, and under what circumstances. We learn that we can talk to some members of the family about a touchy topic, but other topics are off limits. We may identify confidants in whom we can trust and other people we can't. Some families have rules about not talking to certain family members about certain things. These can be called "it'll kill Grandma" rules. People are asked to keep secrets because the news is deemed too shocking for "Grandma" to take in. Someone may actually say, "If you talk about that, it'll kill Grandma," which of course is just a figure of speech. Comments like this reflect communication patterns that help us feel safe emotionally within the family. However, we may find that breaking the old communication rules is crucial to creating a personal life and family dynamics that are healthier. Communication disclosure patterns can create wellness or disease in our families of origin as well as in the organizational systems we join.

Patterns Learned in the Congregation

Joining a congregation involves joining a community with communication rules of its own. For both clergy and laity these communication patterns may be unfamiliar or similar to those in their family of origin. And just like patterns in families of origin, these congregational communication patterns can harm or enhance community life and relationships. Many congregational conflicts result from mismanagement of information; sensitive information is prematurely disclosed or crucial information is withheld or distorted. Too often the patterns of communication in our congregations do more harm than good.

One congregation was almost ripped apart when rumors began about their new priest's sexual orientation. As more and more people talked about the new priest, many strong feelings arose. Some members had spent their lives in family systems that did not talk openly of such things; they would say, "We don't air our dirty laundry." They just wanted the rumors to stop. Others thought that the priest's sexual orientation, behavior, or experience should be private and that any comments about it would appear homophobic and irrelevant to the life and work of the congregation. Some proposed that since God loves everyone regardless of sexual orientation, the congregation should show it was open and nonjudgmental by just dropping the subject. Some members thought that the priest shouldn't remain in the parish if he were bisexual or homosexual. Others argued that the priest could be open about his sexual orientation and courageously pave the way for congregational growth. Most members of the congregation just wanted to know the truth!

When conflicts arise, anxiety and confusion are understandable outcomes. When the conflict is about the clergyperson who normally leads the congregational resolution process, people become even more anxious and disoriented. Who should talk to whom? Should a committee be handling this information? How could leaders put a stop to the rumors and gossip? How does a congregation control information that is this volatile? What if the information is false? When is this escalating conversation in the legal realm of slander or sexual harassment? If the information is deemed to be true, would the priest's confirmation of it have negative consequences on ordination or advancement? True or false, are the rumors creating a hostile work environment? What effect does this communication pattern have on the individual priest, the committee who hired the new priest, other congregational leaders, members of the congregation, and the integrity of the faith messages?

In every situation some people know information and others don't. A dynamic of "insiders" and "outsiders" develops. Individuals may align themselves with different groups in the congregation according to who knows and who doesn't know. How insiders use the information they have is crucial. How they hear, pass on, or embellish the information has the power to resolve or further complicate the situation.

How a congregation handles information may be related to old patterns and relationships within the system. If these patterns are harmful, leaders can change the pattern—to build trust and create a healthier congregation where privacy is defined, secrecy that damages others is eliminated, and respect for difference is appreciated.

Disclosure and the Unique Role of Clergy

Within the clergy role, certain things are simply expected. Clergy and their family members feel tremendous pressure to behave appropriately and be perfect in every way. The expectation that a person's values and behaviors be congruent is greater for clergy than it is for leaders in any other profession. The community as well as the congregation expects congruence between the clergyperson's homily and daily behaviors. This can lead to a clergyperson's hiding supposedly unacceptable behaviors, such as a piercing or tattoo, as well as more harmful behaviors such as excessive drinking or sexual boundary crossing. For example, one pastor in a small town keeps his wine glasses hidden in the garage so that if congregants drop by the parsonage for tea, they won't see wine glasses in the china cabinet.

Complex patterns of communication arise about clergy behaviors, especially regarding sexuality, use of alcohol, public professionalism or lack thereof, and comparison to former clergy in the congregation. The failures or shortcomings of clergy often become secrets protected by both clergy and church leadership. When clergy do things that they feel are unacceptable to the congregation and the community, they often begin to lead double lives—one public and the other hidden. Their hiding to escape the pressures of high expectations placed on them may then lead to secret keeping.

Clergy can never actually step out of the observed role. When they are ordained, they tacitly agree to live in a "fishbowl" where everyone sees into their lives. While doctors give away a measure of privacy when they agree to be on call, clergy give away much more, essentially agreeing to be scrutinized and observed by congregants—and often by community members too. To deal with the fishbowl, clergy monitor their conversations. How much can they disclose, to whom, and when? Managing public versus private information is particularly tricky in denominations where explicit rules exist about sexual behaviors that could, if violated, result in the termination of ordination. For example, a single clergyperson whose date's car is parked outside her home overnight could face serious repercussions.

In a congregational ministry, congregants feel entitled to observe and report on or conceal clergy behavior. More power rests with those leaders who know the most about the clergy in their congregation. In a survey of Presbyterian elders, almost three-quarters of the elders said they would protect personal information about a pastor from the *congregation*—but almost 60 percent felt *they* should know personal information about the pastor. One Presbyterian elder quipped that even if church members should not know personal information about their leaders, they will know it anyway.[1]

The degree to which clergy are affected by this virtual fishbowl often depends on the size of the congregation, its theology, its rural or urban location, and the race and ethnicity of its members. Larger urban congregations provide clergy with more anonymity in their personal lives than small rural congregations where clergy shop at the same stores, are often active in the same clubs, and have children in the same schools as the other townspeople. In some urban congregations, a clergyperson never really retires from his or her congregational family; the relationship between minister and congregants continues long after the official pastoral role is finished. In a small congregation in a rural farming community, Max, a retired pastor, regularly attends worship, influences decisions, and drops by to see former congregants. His behavior is seen as normal. Yet the same behaviors in a suburban parish would be seen as interfering with the ministry of the new clergyperson and the congregation's future. Some clergy serving larger and urban churches have greater freedom to distinguish between private and public life.

Patterns Learned from Religious Teachings

While each congregation has its own communication style and tacit
ground rules for withholding or sharing information, congregations of a given tradition often exhibit communication patterns
based on their religious foundations. Faith traditions create an
understanding of Scripture and of the moral justifications upon
which a congregation bases its decisions to conceal information.
In the early Jewish and Christian traditions, Scripture and life
within the faith community encouraged speaking rather than
concealing information. Neither Jesus nor the Hebrew prophets
ever specifically mentioned confidentiality issues. Because of the
interconnectedness of individuals and their village life, confidentiality may have been a foreign concept to them. Personal struggles,
tragedies, and sins were disclosed publicly rather than being kept
private or confidential. In ancient traditions, confessions were
open and visible. Ezra confessed, wept, and threw himself down
before the house of God and a large crowd (Ezra 10:1). Early faith
leaders like David (1 Chron. 21:16–17) wore sackcloth and fell on
their faces as they publicly confessed their sins. As the Christian
community developed, this tradition of openness continued with
increased emphasis. Brothers and sisters in faith were expected to
know each other well, so that they could hold one another and the
fledgling church accountable to the practices of the new religion.
The community had few boundaries about sharing information.
Aquinas himself declared it sinful to fail to tell the truth when it
ought to be told (yet he also recommended discretion).

Between the second and sixth centuries, the church increasingly formalized its rituals of public confession and the discipline
of wrongdoers. What had been public practice of disclosure and
forgiveness among members of the faith community gradually
shifted to disclosure to a priest and pardons granted by him. Two
dynamics influenced this shift. First, church leaders realized the
high visibility of public confession tended to discourage openness,
and that trend might ultimately affect spiritual health. Second, the

power and authority was centralizing in the ordained priesthood and the institutional church. By the end of the sixth century what had been public confession in the early church became a private communication with the priest and eventually sealed within the tradition.

As the information congregants knew about each other's private lives became more limited, what they knew about church governance and other aspects of church life also became increasingly limited. Over the centuries, the early church's practice of open and equitable sharing of information shifted to patterns of concealing more and more. This historical trend accompanied the amassing of power into hierarchical leadership and the centralization of church governance in Rome. Few parishioners, if any, knew the inner workings of church leadership, church polity, the way clergy were selected and placed in churches or transferred, who members were, or why some members were excommunicated.

The Reformation of the 16th century triggered diverse new approaches to being a Christian community, in particular reclaiming the tradition of the priesthood of all believers. In the polities of the new Protestant churches, leadership was restored to congregants. The reempowerment of laity necessitated that information related to church governance be shared more openly, though the tradition of confidentiality continued.

To this day, Christian communities rely on scriptures that stress the importance of

- truthfulness in all interactions (1 Kings 2:4; 2 Kings 20:3; Pss. 15:2; 26:3; and 51:6; John 8:31–32);
- openly confronting wrongdoing (Matt. 18:15–19);
- speaking the truth lovingly (Eph. 4:15).

Scriptural concepts of truthfulness concern more than telling factual information rather than lying; they also encourage telling the deeper truths that enhance our relationships with God and with one another. Scripture recommends when and what to reveal—and

when to conceal or not to speak (Eccles. 3:7b). Passages forbid mali-
ciousness (Rom. 1:29; Eph. 4:31; 1 Pet. 3:16), slander or fabrication
(Matt. 15:19; Mark 7:22; Rom. 1:30; 2 Cor. 12:20; Eph. 4:31; Col.
3:8; 1 Tim. 3:11 and 6:4; 2 Tim. 3:3; Titus 2:3; 1 Pet. 2:1; Ps. 15:3;
101:5; and 140:11; Prov. 10:18 and 30:10), and gossip (Rom. 1:29;
2 Cor. 12:20; 1 Tim. 5:13; Prov. 20:19; and Ezek. 36:3). The essence of Jewish and Christian sacred texts recommends *not speaking*
information that would inhibit the building up of the community
and the believers themselves (1 Cor. 14:4, 26 and Eph. 4:25–32)
and *speaking* the truth that would contribute to the well-being of
the faith community and the individuals who make it up.

Although both Hebrew and Christian scriptures encourage
truth telling and transparency before God and one another, congregations tend to keep secrets about things they are ashamed of
or afraid to face. They are tempted to place self-interest over truth
telling when the truth is painful or damaging and they hope to
maintain a good image. Sometimes the hope of appearing "perfect
as your heavenly Father is perfect" (Matt. 5:48) promotes secret
keeping about shortcomings. If the goal is not the truth but saving
face or trying to look good, Luke 6:26 warns, "Woe to you when
all speak well of you."

Patterns Learned within Culture

As leaders consider their role as information trustees, they need to
be aware of the different cultures within and beyond their congregations. The congregational culture a person grew up in, generational
issues, socioeconomic status, ethnicity, and ancestry all converge in
the current faith community. Aspects of the culture of our birth and
the cultures that currently surround us will affect our congregation,
as leaders and members are influenced by cultural values, norms,
and standards. In some congregations, the fact that someone died of
AIDS would never be publicly disclosed. In many cultures, whether
or not the bride was a virgin on her wedding night would not be
publicly shared, yet in others the blood from the breaking of the

hymen would be shown to the community and shared as part of a worship celebration.

Cultural Issues Affecting Disclosure

- congregational culture a person grew up in
- generational issues
- socioeconomic status
- ethnicity
- ancestry

Determining what to disclose becomes especially complicated in multigenerational, cross-cultural, or bicultural communities. Between generations privacy rules can change in the culture. At a recent workshop in a local congregation, a teenager announced with pride that she was a lesbian. This announcement was followed by smiles and congratulatory handshakes by some members of the congregation, while others were visibly uncomfortable and remained silent. What and how much is said about sexuality and marriage are particularly bound within cultural norms.

Individual Motivation for Talking Too Much or Too Little

Not only can leaders benefit from recognizing their learned disclosure patterns, but they also benefit from an awareness of their own and other people's motivations behind these processes. The more clarity leaders have about their motivations for disclosure, the less likely they are to disclose something that could harm others or lead to litigation. In high stress situations, information management is even more difficult because leaders can and do make decisions with undue haste. The following two stories illustrate the ways that leaders who are unaware of their motivations can damage themselves and others by mismanaging information.

Talking Too Much

After Denise was called by Oakwood Christian Church to become its senior pastor, she was busily wrapping up her ministry in another state. She had several months before making the transition to Oakwood. The hiring committee appointed an official liaison for Denise, but the first phone calls she received from the congregation came from a woman about her age named Veronica. Veronica was going on a business trip to the area where Denise currently lived and wondered if they could meet for lunch. Denise was pleased and eager to talk about the life of the Oakwood church and agreed to meet Veronica.

Over lunch Veronica made it clear that she hoped that Denise and she would become good friends. She was eager to tell her all of the things she could about Oakwood. Over the few weeks following the lunch, Denise began to confide in Veronica about her stress in the transition, her husband's reluctance to uproot the family, and her concerns about whether or not she had the experience she would need to lead the Oakwood congregation. Unbeknown to Denise, Veronica took this information and spread it throughout the congregation.

Veronica was a member of the hiring and personnel committees of the congregation. At Oakwood, the leaders knew she had been antagonistic toward two previous pastors, and they kept her on the committees so that they would know what she was up to. Harold, who was the appointed liaison to Denise, was so busy working on logistics that he didn't mind Veronica's "friendly" chatting with Denise. The full committee was unaware of the devastation that Veronica's leaks were creating in the parish. Parishioners were already developing negative feelings about Denise's husband, due to his reluctance to be a part of their church. Truths were distorted, and Denise's acknowledged uncertainty was passed throughout the congregation. This made her especially vulnerable to gender stereotyping about women as clergy. Veronica slanted the truth just far enough to lend suspicions about whether or not this would be a good match for the parish.

This story gives us a glimpse into personal motivations for sharing too much information. Denise overdisclosed personal doubts to a parishioner to whom she was supposed to be ministering. Without knowing Veronica, she began sharing personal information that could (and did) damage her reputation before she had even arrived at the parish. Why was she vulnerable to overdisclosure? Denise, like many clergy, was lonely in her vocation. She had few confidants and little time to build friendships outside of her parish obligations. She and her husband were struggling in their marriage, and this too made her vulnerable in sharing with others. She wanted and needed a friend and made an error of judgment by using a relatively unknown parishioner as a confidant.

In hindsight she realized that she should have filtered all communication with Veronica from the beginning. Was this a personal relationship? No, theirs was a pastoral, professional relationship. Since Denise was the pastor, they could not be equal. Denise placed herself outside the professional role and actually reversed the roles. Denise was disclosing things that only a trusted, long-tested relationship of two equals could protect. These things might have been discussed more productively with a colleague or therapist.

Why did Veronica share the information? Veronica had a negative reputation in the congregation that she was trying to improve. Her motivations, perhaps unconscious, were to raise her own esteem in the eyes of her peers in the parish and to relieve her guilt for treating the other pastors poorly by providing this pastor with some supposed support. Veronica had one further motivation. She wasn't happy with the direction the past pastors had set for the congregation. She thought that by getting into Denise's inner circle of friends, she would have power to derail ideas that she felt weren't right for the congregation.

Harold, the committee liaison, also handled the information inappropriately by giving up his power and authority as official liaison for Denise's transition to Oakwood. He was just too busy and overworked to function effectively in that role. Even when he witnessed the result of Veronica's gossip, he avoided confrontation with her, telling himself that she was just being her old self again. He didn't challenge her behavior because he wanted to protect his own image as a good man, to avoid increased friction with Veronica, and to dodge his accountability in the situation. Fear and self-protection were underlying motivations for Denise, Veronica, and Harold, and image management was an active component of their behavior.

Lacking awareness of the power of information, Denise disclosed too much too soon to a person she barely knew, which limited her effectiveness in ministry at her new church from the outset. Similar ignorance about motivations behind overdisclosure blindsided the personnel committee, creating a rocky beginning to what otherwise would have been an excellent relationship between the parish and the pastor.

Talking Too Little

Sometimes talking too little is also a problem for clergy and lay leaders. When June and Stan arrived at Rabbi Joshua's office for a counseling appointment, June was visibly upset. June and Stan were in their late 40s, and Joshua had married them just a few months earlier. Their new family included June's two teenaged daughters. In the protection of the rabbi's office, June told Stan and Joshua that her 16-year-old had accused Stan of putting his hands on her breasts when they were in the car alone. She wanted to know if this was true. Stan became red in the face and very agitated, claiming that he had done no such thing and that the girl was a little tramp who was just trying to get the family off-base so that she could go out with her boyfriend and have sex. Stan said that she had hated him since he had joined the family and was just trying to bust up their new marriage. June grew silent and sullen. He accused June of believing her daughter rather than him and announced that they were leaving the counseling session and would not talk about it anymore. He stood, and they both left the office.

Rabbi Joshua was left with a complex situation and decisions to make about his disclosure or silence regarding the content of the session. He may have been motivated to keep the situation quiet for several reasons, including his professional role, his personal relationship with Stan, and his own upbringing in which silence was kept about family issues that were shaming. Stan may have donated generously to the synagogue and Joshua didn't want to jeopardize that funding. Joshua may have been Stan's buddy at Rotary Club and wanted to protect Stan's reputation in the community. The rabbi may have wanted to feel that the marriage he had blessed was a good one and his silence might keep the family intact. He may have wanted to protect his own reputation in the face of Stan's power in the community.

Joshua believed that pastoral confidences should be protected. As a rabbi he felt that he had the authority to make decisions about what he heard in his office. Religious polity and state law must both be considered, however. Each faith tradition has its own guidelines about confidentiality and abuse reporting, and Joshua was unaware that as a Reformed Jew his rabbinical guidelines required reporting all child abuse suspicions to civil authorities. Whether he was aware of it or not, his responsibility included knowing and following his state's child abuse reporting laws and requirements for clergy. In most states Joshua would be legally mandated to call child protective services with the information he had heard.

In violation of state law and his faith tradition, Joshua decided to keep the incident quiet. He rationalized that this was a minor incident and that it was better to keep the family together if possible. He was further motivated toward silence by the tremendous incongruence he felt between his image of Stan as a good provider and a community and congregational leader and this detail about Stan's private life. Joshua thought that if he called the child protective services agency, despite its assurances of confidentiality, Stan would surely suspect Joshua was the one who had reported the teenager's comment. He was also motivated by rumors that child protective services in his area were ineffective, and he supposed that he could provide more helpful intervention himself.

Joshua's decision to keep quiet had disastrous results. June divorced Stan a few months later, and when the abuse allegation was proved to be true, June sued the congregation for Joshua's failure to file a report and protect her daughter.

To Tell or Not to Tell?

These two examples reflect decisions to manage information by disclosing too much or withholding what is crucial to share. Mismanagement of information can hurt individuals and congregations, though the harm is rarely intentional. Individuals usually think their decisions are appropriate, though a good number of them are motivated by the desire to protect themselves from pain or discomfort rather than wise discernment. While disclosing too much or disclosing too little seem like different problems, similar motivations influence both behaviors. The box below illustrates the underlying components of both problems.

Individual Motivations for Disclosing Information

When individuals decide what information they will disclose, as well as when and to whom, they may hope to

1. avoid making a mistake because of uncertainty about what to do, inexperience, or lack of training, guidelines, or policies;
2. protect their self-esteem (or maintain a good image, reputation, or revenue);
3. reduce feelings of guilt, shame, or vulnerability;

4. maintain significant relationships that might be damaged or enhanced by the information;
5. get love, affection, or attention;
6. maintain power and control;
7. dodge accountability;
8. avoid the discomfort of ambiguity, change, or psychological disequilibrium;
9. protect someone or something else, perhaps the congregation itself.

The following commonplace story illustrates each motivation listed in the box above. Pastor Jeff often preached about how much he suffered because of his wife and children's medical and emotional problems. If people listened closely, they realized that he was sharing personal information about family that should have been private; the congregation had neither the right nor the need to know the stories that were his wife's and children's to tell, not his. Though experienced in the pulpit, he lacked training on appropriate professional boundaries and had no clergy ethics policy to guide his choices about what to say to whom (Motivation 1). His self-esteem was too dependent on the success and fame of his church and its impressive attendance was slowly dwindling. By pointing out his wife's and children's shortcomings, he distracted attention away from his own, thus protecting his self-esteem (Motivation 2). He had a reputation to protect and reduced his feelings of guilt and shame about the church's decline by scapegoating his family (Motivation 3). Unfortunately his loose sharing of family information harmed relationships with his wife and children, although it enhanced his relationships with most parishioners who were spellbound by his sermons and by his generous openness about his struggles (Motivation 4). They surrounded him with affection, attention, and support: "Poor man! How can he lead the church with such challenges at home?" (Motivation 5). His oratory power in the pulpit coupled with his ability to manipulate other people into protecting him assured his control of the congregation (Motivation 6). This manipulation helped him dodge accountability for his failure to lead the church with vision and integrity (Motivation 7). His inner sense of failure and his outer presentation of himself didn't match; to avoid internal change he spent his time evaluating and complaining about others (Motivation 8). He was trying to divert the church from recognizing his ineffective leadership and avoid a public termination. So he used a style of disclosure he presumed would protect the reputation of the church by portraying it as a place of down-to-earth, "real" preaching (Motivation 9).

The pastor put himself in a vulnerable and precarious situation, however. His parishioners lost their trust in his ability to hold information appropriately. They were hesitant to share their personal experiences with him for fear that he would spread those too. And the energy of the church became more focused on coddling him than on living out the faith.

Group Motivations for Disclosing Too Much or Too Little

A congregation is a group of individuals, all of whom have motivations and communication patterns. Individuals disclose too little or too much to keep themselves safe from pain; they also try to protect their treasured organizations. Individuals tend to join congregations that support their beliefs and attitudes rather than challenge them, so congregations become filled with people trying to maintain both their personal self-image and the group image. The motivations discussed above become amplified as protection of oneself enmeshes with desire for the congregational system to stay intact and aligned with that individual's belief. When an individual must decide whether to reveal or to conceal information, the strength of that person's motivation multiplies as he or she joins other individuals to form a group.

Robert and Jack had been partners for 10 years when they joined a neighborhood congregation. Moved by the welcome they received, they dropped by the pastor's office and asked Dwayne if he would marry them at church. Dwayne agreed that would be right in the eyes of God to bless their union and confirm their promises to each other, but he would need to take the decision to the committee of elders at their next meeting.

Pastor Dwayne brought the subject up to the board of elders. Silence filled the room for a while. Then a man stood up and addressed the dozen people in the room who had been his longtime friends. He told them that his middle son, Gus, was gay and that he had had a hard time coming to grips with it. He had never told any of them about this because of his own shame and confusion about it. Now, he said, he longed for the day when his son would find a partner and be legally married.

The group was again silent. Then, one after another, group members began telling stories about how homosexuality issues had been dealt with (or not) in their families of origin. They were often moved to tears. Most of them felt ready to move forward with the service, and some articulated the gospel call to justice as a reason to do so. Only one woman said that she would never agree to it, because she was afraid that it would divide the congregation. The pastor had been hoping that the vote would be unanimous, but with a strong majority they voted to proceed.

This small group of people fell into a dynamic known as "groupthink." In groupthink, people who are motivated by emotions and a desire to release tension join together to take an action that in the heat of the moment seems wise but might not be when the action is more rationally considered. Groupthink is a process of moving too quickly before all issues are raised and all people have been heard. Groupthink is not the same as consensus building or a process of collective decision making. In groupthink people may feel that everyone agrees, but in fact the group has simply moved so quickly that the energy or enthusiasm of the moment has driven the decision. Groupthink reinforces other motivations in the group, for example, the motivation to be liked by peers and to be seen as similar to other members in the group.

When the elders reconvened the next month, they decided not to say anything about the upcoming ceremony to the whole congregation. They would treat the service as they would any other marriage ritual, except it would not be included in the church's official records. This worked well until a member of the congregation overheard two of her friends talking about the service. This member disapproved of gay marriage and was irate that the congregation hadn't voted whether or not Pastor Dwayne could perform the ceremony.

Dwayne and the elders were motivated to protect the congregation under the old adage, "What they don't know won't hurt them." This really means that the committee was conflict avoidant; they didn't want their long-term friends and members challenging them about their decision.

Hoping to protect their pastor's reputation as a mainstream preacher who appealed to a broad constituency, the board of elders didn't talk about the commitment service to anyone in the community. If others thought the pastor was an activist for gay rights, the congregation's image in the community would possibly change too.

Some of them kept silent to maintain the status quo and to avoid change that could disrupt the peace. If the word got out that the elders had approved this action, what would that mean for the biblical and theological beliefs of the congregation? Would the congregation be a focal point for a debate about homosexuality and the Bible? Would gays and lesbians, bisexuals, and transgendered people flock to the congregation and change its nature and mission? Would the congregation's "mainstream" reputation in the community change? Motivations to maintain the status quo, to look good to others, to avoid conflict, and to protect congregational identity are all operative in this situation. They led to the decision to keep the information silent.

That decision backfired. When people learned about the service via the informal communication networks among them, many of them were furious. They felt betrayed both by the fact that they had not been included in what to them was a major decision and by the assumption that the pastor was doing things under the table that they had a right to know about. When the news spread throughout the congregation, many members left. They not only disagreed with the idea of the service but they also felt disenfranchised by a board of elders who did not represent them. By the time discussions took place about relevant scripture and theology, people were too angry and hurt to engage in a learning process. Instead they discredited the entire leadership.

Had the elders or the pastor considered the larger context of their decision beyond their initial groupthink, their decision to conduct the service might have been the same, but their choice about including the congregation in their decision might have been different. No matter how well intentioned, the elders failed to recognize the damage that would be created by their lack of disclosure. What they saw as private, others saw as secretive. What they saw as a situation respectfully handled, others saw as a betrayal of trust by those in power.

In some congregations, nondisclosure becomes a pattern. These congregations keep the system in check by stigmatizing anyone who tells the truth within the system. At every annual meeting in one congregation, when members are poised to vote on the budget, an accountant stands up and complains that the senior pastor's pay is three times that of the associate. Why does he do that? He knows that the finance committee combines the salaries in its report to the congregation to hide the unjust skew in pay. The pastor claims that individual salaries should be private; however, all except the two pastoral staff salaries are individual line items in the budget. But the actual associate pastor's salary stays a protected secret each year, and parishioners simply dismiss the "old curmudgeon" as being the problem and make fun of his outspoken questioning at every meeting.

Individuals who refuse to keep secrets and instead tell truths that others wish to keep hidden usually become ostracized. In congregations this ostracizing of truth tellers keeps secrets within the congregation from leaking out and discourages others from speaking up. Those who disclose what has been hidden information often bear the wrath of others, so it is not surprising that many people are motivated to remain silent to protect themselves among friends, colleagues, or fellow parishioners.

When a lay staff member was dismissed for viewing pornography on his office computer, congregational leaders hushed up the situation. The departing staff member was willing to tell the whole congregation the real reason for his leaving but was strongly discouraged from doing so. His computer had been on a desk in an open area in the office complex, so to admit that he had a sexual addiction problem could have created suspicion that youth, children, and others could have seen the pornography he was viewing. The congregation's lawyer had him sign a gag order upon his departure.

In another congregation a departing pastor we will call Joan was believed to have a serious alcohol problem. The personnel committee chairperson wanted to tell the judicatory staff so that Joan could receive help, but those who feared the church would be sued for defaming the pastor's character told the chairperson not to go to the judicatory. What if the former pastor could not find another job or the information caused her to lose her ordination? When the chairperson decided to go forward and disclose within the parish and with judicatory staff the reasons for Joan's dismissal, people became nasty toward the chairperson for "spreading around the news" and for "shaming the poor woman."

Similar motivations apply whether the congregation has a pattern of overly tight boundaries of silence and secrets or a lack of boundaries where everything is shared and known by everyone and no privacy exists. The motivations are, in a sense, all about the desire to protect the congregation from falling into conflict or, worse, dividing or closing down.

Congregational Motivation
Related to Disclosing Information

When congregations decide what information they will disclose, as well as when and to whom, they may hope to

- portray clergy and the congregation in the best light;
- maintain the status quo and avoid change;
- enhance belonging;
- honor the philosophy of niceness: "If you don't have anything nice to say, don't say anything at all."

Congregations will also exhibit the same motivations as individuals. See the list on pages 22–23.

The desire to protect ourselves as individuals and as a group motivates our disclosure decisions. No one wants to harm another person, a family, or a congregation. No one wants to harm himself or herself either. But protecting *every*one is nearly impossible. Leaders can avoid patterns of dysfunction by learning to recognize and then discuss their motivations.

Remember the children's saying, "Sticks and stones can break my bones, but words will never hurt me"? Words can hurt. The examples of wounds caused by words, or the lack of them, are found throughout this book. Pastors leave parishes and sometimes parish ministry on the basis of communication patterns that wound. Whole churches shut down. To grow spiritually and numerically, vital congregations, leaders, and clergy can and must become aware of harmful disclosure patterns and begin to name and explore the motivations that lie beneath them.

Chapter 2

Concealing Information

In every conversation we choose what to conceal and what to reveal. What we choose to conceal about ourselves can be safely tucked away as part of our background, memory, and character. French philosopher and theologian Paul Tournier argues that privacy and the concealment of certain personal information is what defines our individuality.[1] When free to keep certain dreams, frustrations, failures, or soul work private, we can protect our inner space without coercion. We each determine what personal and private information to share as a way to keep ourselves free from unwanted access or vulnerability. This privacy contributes to our individuality.

Privacy or Secrecy?

For many of us, the distinction between what is private and what is secret is difficult to determine. Privacy defines our character and protects our inner life. We *choose* to keep certain information private. But not all information we withhold from others is private. Some is information we have felt pressured by others to keep to ourselves. Perhaps we were threatened with rejection or retaliation if we disclosed it. That information becomes a secret when it is withheld from others who need to know it. We keep secrets both from ourselves and from others because we have deemed the content too terrible, too harmful, or too anxiety producing to be revealed. Shame and fear charge the information with emotion.

Fear, shame, or intimidation may send some stories underground when they reflect badly on the reputation of an individual within a congregation or the whole congregation. If not surfaced, those stories turn into secrets that affect leadership and the general well-being of the congregation. Secrets cloud vision. Without transparency of crucial information, guiding the congregation is like "swimming through muddy water," as one pastor at a congregational development workshop lamented. "Or playing cards without the full deck," another chimed in.

A pastor experiencing financial difficulty chose to keep his private struggle to himself. However, his financial issues began to interfere with his ministry. Without explaining his personal challenges to church leaders, he began to avoid dealing with church finances, never went on vacation, and preached more frequently about the evils of money. When others noticed and commented about these changed behaviors, he felt increasingly threatened that his money problems would be exposed. His shame and fear increased the energy with which he shielded his privacy. But in truth, his private information had become a secret. Keeping a secret is more emotionally charged than protecting private matters. The effort required to maintain a secret, monitor the responses of others, direct conversations away from the secret, and put on a false front when directly challenged about it is emotionally draining and interpersonally damaging.

As the pastor's ministry deteriorated, church leaders needed some explanation for his anxiety and behavior—but his secret left them confused and frustrated. The information he withheld from church leaders was no longer private because it affected not just the pastor's life but also the life of the congregation. His silence and behavior jeopardized the well-being of the church and, if continued, could have cost him his position as pastor. Without engaging in secrecy, the pastor still could have maintained his privacy. The church leaders *only* needed to be told that the appropriate committee (mutual ministry, personnel, or pastoral relations) was working with the pastor to resolve the problems. Members of that particular committee needed *only* to know the basic issue, not personal details, and how they might help the pastor address his distress and the behavior it precipitated. Without sacrificing his privacy, the pastor could have shared the information that was directly affecting his public ministry.

Just as privacy gives us the power to define ourselves, secrecy and power also intertwine—but negatively. Guarding a secret requires such attention and energy that the secret has power over its keeper. Protecting a secret can subtly and unconsciously control the secret keeper's life.

Paradoxically, when we hold a secret, it has power over us but we also have power over those who do not know the information. Ethicist Sissela Bok explains that to keep a secret from someone else is to intentionally hide that information and to "block information about it or evidence of it from reaching that person . . . to prevent him [or her] from learning it, and thus from possessing it, making use of it, or revealing it."[2] That power may be used to control or dominate individuals and congregations, without the secret holder having to experience shame or accountability for any damage the secret creates. When certain individuals or groups withhold crucial information, faith leaders may never know why certain problems keep limiting their congregation's vitality. In essence, secret keepers rather than elected leaders run the church.

Secrets Congregations Keep

Individual congregants keep secrets, their faith leaders keep secrets, and whole congregations keep secrets. What kinds of secrets do congregations keep? What stories of the past are hidden from new members? Sometimes the whole community knows about something that no one in the congregation ever talks about publicly. As pastor Shelly was moving out of a parsonage where she had lived for five years, one of her neighbors came by to help her pack. "Well now," she said to Shelly, "it's a good thing you are getting out alive!" "What?" Shelly asked. "Why wouldn't I be?"

"Oh, didn't you know? The last two pastors made it out alive too, but the one before that hung himself in the basement." Shelly never knew. She was astonished that news of such significance was covered up for the five years of her tenure as pastor of the congregation. Why were they all so silent about it?

Wherever shame and embarrassment are lurking, a secret is also likely to be lurking. Wherever a secret lurks in a congregational system, underlying distortions of power and control, anxiety about decision making, rigid in-group and out-group structures, lack of trust in leadership authority, and other unhealthy dynamics may be at work. Unfortunately, congregations keep secrets about all kinds of subjects—finances, clergy violations of trust, so-called special relationships within the congregation, bad decisions, and more.

Secrets about Money

Every family, and every church family, handles money differently. Who can know about finances, who talks about them, who makes decisions about them are all dependent on the history and culture of a particular congregation. Many families and many congregational families think "it's just not right" to talk about money, so few people in congregations talk about money comfortably. Financial conversations go underground or become diffused, diluted, or convoluted. Secrets abound about crucial fiduciary information, such as congregational indebtedness, embezzlement by staff or clergy, pledges, endowment resources, "borrowing" of funds by leadership or staff, and insurance coverage.

For example, the chairperson of the board of First Church brokered secret financial deals in order to launch a new building program. He borrowed large sums of money from individuals for the project without informing the congregation of those loans. The secret was revealed when the sums weren't repaid as promised. The lending parishioners felt swindled and sued the congregation. The congregation almost lost its building because it had such a limited amount of liability insurance (another secret), and the lawsuit exceeded its resources. The trustee who had signed the insurance renewal papers knew the policy limits were too low. He had hoped to impress the other board members with the savings he had made, but the savings and the secret came with a significant price tag.

Some money secrets relate to how certain funds are spent. One pastor acquired generous donations to the church and told the donors the money was going into an endowment fund. Soon thereafter, without involving the elected lay leaders or the donors in the decision, the pastor moved those funds into the general budget and used them to cover current bills. When clergy or lay leaders handle money unethically or secretively and are later discovered, most congregations tend to quietly ask for a resignation rather than ask for accountability and appropriate consequences—even when the leader's actions constitute embezzlement.

Sometimes the secret is about how resources are raised, managed, and allocated. When committee members don't know how to access the money they need for programs, their mission may come to a grinding halt, as in the following example. After six years, a Midwest pastor still couldn't understand how the finances were handled at his church. And no wonder. Money was monitored by the finance committee, the endowment committee, the investments committee, the stewardship committee, the special funds committee, the budget committee, and the pastor and staff salary committee—seven committees in all! Each financial committee had a distinct function and met frequently, but the committees only met together once a year at budget planning time. This chaotic, inefficient financial management protected the secret that in truth, the church's patriarch, Mr. Hadley, made most decisions about expenditure of funds. He founded the church, he gave the most money, and he expected to maintain his power, regardless of whether he was elected to an official position.

When the program committees at First Church needed money to accomplish ministry goals, they became bogged down in the church structure as they tried to access available funds. How to get the money they needed, how much was available, and whether or not they could raise more of it were all secretive processes, leaving committee chairpersons and the pastor confused and frustrated. The protection of money had taken precedence over the mission and outreach of the congregation. Having seven committees handle finances was like putting the money in several vaults to which no one had keys—when the secret key was actually Mr. Hadley. Certainly any congregation dependent on any particular donor has numerous challenges, not the least of which is the tendency to give that member extra voice or vote in decision making about the mission, personnel, and budget of the parish. While First Church faced more challenges than most, every congregation has its share of financial secrets.

Secrets are contagious. One secret in a congregation can foster other secrets. When secret keeping becomes habitual, it can become like a virus that infects multiple areas of congregational life—like a hiring secret at Temple Beth El that put the members at risk of abuse and the congregation as a whole at risk of losing its insurance coverage. A particularly charming and gifted man was the top candidate for the senior rabbi position. In the course of checking the rabbi's background, the chairperson learned that prior sexual abuse allegations had been made against the rabbi and that he had been convicted of sexual misconduct by rabbinical authorities. The chairperson shared that information with her committee, but she chose not to share letters from women who alleged the rabbi had recently been sexually inappropriate with them. She also knew from her own investigations—but did not tell the committee—that hiring this rabbi jeopardized the congregation's insurance policy, because the company would not insure congregations who knowingly hired clergy or staff who were convicted of sexual boundary violations. Although the rabbi was clearly a danger to the women in the congregation, the congregation hired him. Later, in its annual audit, the insurance carrier discovered who the congregation had hired and promptly cancelled the insurance, sending the lay leaders into shock and a scramble to find new and now much more expensive coverage.

Secrets about Donors

Knowledge of congregational members' potential and actual giving is especially powerful data, and therefore debates arise about who should know that information. Donations to ministry aren't private because someone in addition to the donor knows about them. At least one other person knows the amount of a donor's pledge and giving, but who? Does the pastor have access to that information? Do the stewardship committee members know who gives and how much is given? Or does the whole congregation know?

When an associate pastor's salary was funded by one donor in a congregation, the job itself was at risk, but neither the associate nor most other parishioners had any idea the funding was linked to a specific donor. The donor had ultimate power over the associate pastor both because he gave all the money and because that arrangement was secret. A few church trustees were in on the secret, which gave them power over church members who were never informed about the arrangement. The associate couldn't figure out why one man treated him so differently, as if the man were his boss—but he later found out. When the donor became angry about the associate's desires to add a new contemporary worship service, the donor withdrew funds for the salary, and the church had no choice but to eliminate the position.

Anonymous gifts are not truly anonymous because someone in the congregation has to cash the check or process the donation. The donor simply asks that his or her name not be publicized. But so-called anonymous gifts can promote secrets if the donor assumes some authority or exerts pressure over use of the money but doesn't want to be found out and held accountable. Truly anonymous gifts have no ongoing strings attached. An anonymous donation for a new organ doesn't become a right to select the music played on Sundays. Who pesters the organist and why may be a secret as well as a power dynamic that limits congregational growth.

When donor names or gift levels are withheld from the clergy, problems may arise. The pastor may know less than lay leaders about the financial status of the congregation, the giving potential of current or new members, or problems that have arisen with individual congregants that they express by withdrawing donations. Many clergy do not want to know specific donation information at all; some clergy ask only to know who gives but not how much, or to know significant changes in giving levels—either up or down. One pastor, responsible for recommending candidates to serve on his board, said he wanted to ensure that everyone he nominated actually pledged to the church. Another pastor watched the giving patterns of his parishioners throughout the year and from year to year as indicators of the need for pastoral care.

Rev. Andrews enthusiastically embraced the long-range planning team's suggestions for future direction of his congregation, assuming the team thoroughly analyzed the church's current financial picture. Because he didn't have that information, he trusted that the team had studied historical giving patterns and endowment information. The church's trustees only let their pastors know the basic annual budget but no more detail, supposedly to avoid micromanagement by the clergy. Rev. Andrews naively charged ahead, hiring two staff, printing thousands of fliers advertising the church, and making other expensive expenditures at the team's recommendation. The sparkling Web site, handsome new logo, and youthful energetic staff implied a dazzling congregational life.

Just six months later, Rev. Andrews said he felt like a drum major whose band had refused to march in the parade. All the enthusiasm had been purchased or fabricated instead of fueled by church members. The hired staff had taken over the work of volunteers who had vanished and burned out. Something was amiss, but Rev. Andrews couldn't put his finger on it until a banker friend from Rotary met him for coffee. The banker admitted that it was illegal for him to say anything about the church's accounts, but he felt compelled to warn the pastor that by his estimation the church couldn't last another eight months. Apparently the few congregational leaders responsible for financial planning had been so frightened that the church would die that over the years they kept its slowly depleting funds and donor information secret from the other lay and ordained leaders. Such secrets obviously limit leadership effectiveness, set the stage for potential misuse of power and position, and create secrecy among the membership.

Some congregational secrets involve special donors whose friends in the congregation can call on them to fund pet projects. Such a congregational secret backfired when a new pastor stumbled onto part of a secret and used the information without consulting others. Early in his new position as pastor, Andy heard a secret from a lay leader: Marla, a donor at First Presbyterian Church had access to a large family endowment and loved music. So Andy visited Marla and spoke of his dream of having a grand piano in the sanctuary. He told her that the piano would allow them to use music that would appeal to a younger generation and grow the congregation with new families. To his delight, she gave him a check that very day to purchase a piano. But when he announced the gift at the next worship committee meeting, he could tell that something was wrong. The committee's response was silence and nervous fidgeting. At last someone spoke up and said, "We've been getting bids on replacing the stops on the pipe organ, and the work will cost almost as much as a grand piano. Marla gives one gift of that size every year, and now you've taken it away from us." Unwittingly, Andy had interfered with a decade-old pattern, a secret kept by the worship committee: Marla made an annual donation, and the worship committee determined how her gift would be used.

The angry worship committee claimed Andy was against organ music and didn't care about the music the older members loved. In truth, their anger stemmed from his discovery of the Marla secret and his new knowledge about and access to money.

Had all the information about donors been transparent to him, Andy could have acted alongside the committee and prevented the repercussions of his talking directly to Marla. But in a congregation of secrets, Andy had acted secretively too. Instead there should have been much broader conversation among leaders about worship and music priorities and ways to fund them.

The more a clergyperson knows about funding sources and patterns, the more clergy can work alongside lay leaders who also know the giving patterns and potential of a congregation. Also, the more a clergyperson knows about funding, the more effectively he or she will be able to guide the mission and ministry of the congregation. When clergy and lay leaders remain uninformed of trends, such as the giving levels of persons by age and demographics, they cannot plan for a financially viable future. For example, in many congregations, more than 50 percent of their funding comes from those who are 70 years and older. Younger donors may not have developed the practice of supporting their congregation financially. Knowing the trends within the congregation assists key lay leaders in the process of fund development. However, when that information becomes a secret leaders keep from one another or their clergy, other secrets are likely and congregational health is jeopardized.

A key ingredient in a congregation's decisions on these issues is not solely who will know donor data but also, does the donor know who knows? Transparent leadership requires donors knowing who will have information about their pledge, how it will be tracked, and who they can call to get an update on their giving. In some congregations everyone has access to the records and is told that prior to solicitation. In these congregations, if someone wants to make a gift anonymously, how will that be handled? The clearer the congregation can be about these issues, the more ethically they will handle financial confidences.

Secrets about Personnel

Clergy and most laity have limited training in personnel management and tend to assume that everything related to personnel issues
should be kept from the wider congregation. Much unintentional
damage is caused by confusing appropriate confidentiality with
keeping secrets about the reasons for staff departures or the hiring
or discipline of certain staff or volunteers.

When Mark hired a part-time director of youth outreach, he
chose Rhonda, an old friend from his years at Forest High School.
Rhonda was enthusiastic, had a master's degree in education, and
was well qualified to lead the youth and children's ministry. A few
months after he had hired her, Mark returned to his high school
reunion and found himself in an uncomfortable conversation.
An old friend passed him a soda and said casually as if it didn't
matter, "Hey, I hear you hired Rhonda to do youth work at your
church. That's pretty gutsy!" Mark asked, "Oh, really? Why?" The
friend, realizing Mark was clueless, became flustered and mumbled
something about her felony sex offense in college. Mark asked
more questions. To his surprise, he learned that Rhonda had been
convicted of participating in sexual activity with a minor. The circumstances were vague but involved a fraternity party when she
was a graduate student, was drinking too much, and had sex with
an underage student whom she had thought was over 18. Now 35-
years-old and the mother of two children, Rhonda was far from
her past and, of course, didn't want anyone to know about it.

Mark consulted the pastor, and the two of them decided to
simply ask Rhonda to resign from her position and keep the
historical information secret. This backfired when a father in the
congregation who worked for child protective services happened
across Rhonda's name on the state's list of registered sex offenders.
Some offenses that people might consider relatively minor and far
in the past may still result in someone having to register as an offender many years after the incident. The father didn't know the
details of her offense, but he did know that she had been meeting

with his daughter and other teens at the church. He began to tell everyone he could about her conviction and about the congregation's cover up, which he was afraid could have led to youth or children being in danger.

This situation involving information in the public record may have been better handled, with Rhonda informing others of her story before her employment or explaining as part of her resignation why she was stepping down from her position. Or with Rhonda's permission, Mark or the minister could have told the story on her behalf and then worked with leadership to determine the wisdom of her continued employment. Her story could have become a teaching tool about the dangers of binge drinking and sex without sobriety. The idea that Rhonda would participate in a more open process of information sharing about her status presumes that Rhonda had a good deal of courage and self-acceptance. It also presumes that she, her husband, and her children all knew about the situation and were prepared to deal with the onslaught of questions, glances, or gossip that would swirl around the family.

Rhonda's story raises difficult questions related to managing personnel issues. What should be kept confidential when handling personnel issues? While personnel laws vary from state to state, an employer typically cannot reveal personnel information other than start and end dates of employment. When they are called to give a reference, employers have become more careful about disclosing reasons for termination or even the good things about an employee's work.

Sometimes employees are asked to keep silent about their own work-related issues. Staff may be asked to keep something a secret under the guise of confidentiality. When an associate pastor was asked to resign for personality differences with the senior minister, he was offered three months pay and benefits if he pretended his resignation was voluntary. If he told others he was dismissed, he would receive only his salary to the end of the first month. Staff may be asked to keep personnel issues private, but when coerced financially they are actually being bribed to keep secrets.

Silencing staff from telling their own stories—whether about something they have experienced or observed—is clearly unethical. When an associate rector was asked to resign from a large church in Houston, the personnel chairperson insisted that she could not say anything to anyone about the fact that she was terminated without cause. The associate rector was told that she could be hired and fired at will, that she was to pack her boxes and leave by the end of the day, and that speaking to anyone in the congregation about her termination would be met with a legal challenge. Her discovery of financial impropriety on the part of the senior rector had triggered such an abrupt reaction; silencing her protected that secret.

One church was left reeling after a secretary, three other staff members, and two associate pastors resigned over a three-year period. Each of the six wrote a letter to the congregation explaining the reasons for his or her resignation. But before circulation, each resignation letter was edited by the senior pastor, who implied or fabricated inaccurate reasons for the resignation. Because of the senior pastor's spin-doctoring, neither the governing board nor the congregation heard about the senior pastor's abusive treatment of staff, which had created an impossible work environment.

In another congregation, when an assistant rector was asked to resign because he used an office computer for Internet chat room conversations and to view adult pornography, the congregation's senior rector decided the congregation should not be told the specific reason for the forced resignation. The personnel committee chairperson simply said that the staff person left because he had engaged in behaviors deemed incompatible with pastoral leadership. The committee also gathered the other members of the staff and told them not to say anything more about the reasons for dismissal.

Sarah, one of the secretaries, however, had seen the assistant rector misusing the computer on several occasions and was uncomfortable with the idea that he could be transferred to work in another Episcopal parish, only to repeat the behavior. Did she have the right to talk about what she witnessed? Sarah believed she did.

The situation became increasingly tense and uncomfortable when she refused, as she said, "to be gag ordered about this!" She decided that she would not keep silent and told her friends in the parish, the chairperson of the education committee, and office coworkers. The personnel chairperson contacted a lawyer in the congregation, and they sent Sarah a letter asking for her resignation for having slandered the good reputation of the assistant rector. Instead of arguing her case in court, she chose to reduce her stress and the backlash from telling the truth and resigned.

The desire to protect an individual's reputation often conflicts with the need for open dialogue and healing within the whole congregation. In the story of Sarah and the assistant rector, the priest's reputation wasn't the only thing the secret protected. The congregation had known of the priest's sexual addiction, had asked him to sign a written contract not to use the computer at his office for pornography on the Internet, and was therefore in greater danger of being sued for its failure to act on its knowledge of the risk of harm. The threat of a lawsuit against Sarah was an attempt to divert attention away from the incident and the congregation as a whole.

Personnel issues must be carefully reviewed in consultation with an attorney. State laws differ about the levels of confidentiality in personnel issues, and some laws apply to congregations while others do not. Written comments about someone that aren't true are libelous; spoken untruths are slanderous. Libel and slander may still occur if it can be proved that the information disclosed is true but was spoken or communicated in writing with the intent to harm the other person. The point could be argued that Sarah had not slandered anyone but had simply spoken the truth of what she witnessed on her job. She told of her observations not to harm the assistant priest but to provide an opportunity to protect others from future potential harm.

Lawyers who handle such cases have to consider specific practices of ministry within the particular religious organization, along with state and federal case law regarding employment issues.

(Much more will be said about legal issues in chapter 7.) Tension naturally develops between the common legal advice to keep all personnel issues completely confidential and the transparency necessary in congregations for effective leadership and governance, healing when a staff member leaves, and problem resolution. When choosing between disclosure and concealment, the consequences have to be fully explored. Secrecy can be as dangerous as boundless disclosure.

Secrets about Former Clergy and Members

Arriving at a new parish, many incoming clergy learn congregational secrets from their predecessors—information the judicatory staff or search committee never mentioned but should have. The leadership transition itself seems to provide permission for people to tell stories they previously kept to themselves. Stories may surface about a former pastor's sexual boundary violations, about his or her having an inappropriate so-called special relationship with one of the parishioners, about his or her continuing to contact some of the members in spite of denominational rules not to, or suggesting the clergyperson had a drinking problem that had affected his or her work. The secret information can tumble out of people and be plopped in the lap of the new person. How this information should be handled is particularly tricky.

A new clergyperson could spend a good deal of time researching whether or not such stories are really true, so some clergy just ignore them. They may assume that even if the stories are true, as long as they remain unacknowledged or undisturbed in people's memories, the stories will remain secret—and safe. The problem with this strategy is that stories about leaders rarely are truly secret; they just aren't discussed openly. Most congregants know stories about past wounds and abuses. The hairdresser in town, the auto mechanic down on Main Street, and others often know stories about unethical behaviors on the part of clergy and lay leaders, that supposedly are hidden from public view. Parking lot conversations, telephone calls, and e-mails keep old stories circulating unofficially. Even while the secrets are being spread around informally underground, the pretense of containing this information can undermine the health of the congregation by distorting open communication, hampering the integration of new members into the faith community, and limiting the current clergyperson's effectiveness.

Clergy often bump into secrets that individuals or families in the congregation hold. Margaret was a member of Cameron Valley Church for years and her husband served on the board of trustees. If you asked anyone in the congregation, you would hear glowing reports about all that the family has done in the past 25 years of leadership—but you wouldn't hear about concerns related to Margaret's drinking. When Pastor Sue went to their home to visit Margaret and her husband, they trusted her with the explanation that Margaret had been recently hospitalized with liver failure due to Margaret's lifelong struggle with alcoholism. Pastor Sue had provided a sense of safety in the conversation, and therefore Margaret and her husband disclosed her alcoholism without either Sue or the family discussing the limits of the information.

Sue felt good that they had confided in her at this difficult time but hadn't realized that the family expected that she not repeat *any* of the conversation about Margaret's illness. A month later when Margaret was hospitalized again, Sue put Margaret on the prayer chain, saying that she was suffering from liver failure. From the family's perspective, Sue might as well have put up a billboard saying, "Margaret is an alcoholic." All of the family's shame surfaced and was directed at the pastor. They didn't want anything about Margaret's illness known for fear of probing questions.

Sue made a clear mistake by not checking with the family to get their permission to place Margaret on the prayer chain. If Pastor Sue had requested and been given permission, she should have clarified the language they wanted her to use. Sue may have thought the family would be helped by having the support of the community, or maybe she just didn't think about the fact that she was revealing a family and a congregational secret. Either way, the information wasn't Sue's secret to share—it was Margaret's. Since Margaret and her husband were more powerful than Sue in the church system, her action precipitated Sue's transfer to another parish.

What do clergy do with the personal information they learn about parishioners? Each bit of information, each story, and each disclosure must be handled with utmost care. Pastoral visits in a home or the pastor's office offer intimate moments in which to share life stories and family secrets. As Sue learned, she needed to ask, "Who owns the story?" What information gained in a pastoral visit can be appropriately repeated in another context? Neither an individual's private information nor secrets hidden in shame are appropriate for clergy to reveal without permission.

Secrets Clergy Keep

Congregations often keep secrets about the struggles or failures of their clergy, but more insidious are the secrets clergy keep about themselves. As stated earlier in the book, the very nature of the pastoral profession leads to the presumption that all aspects of the pastor's life are open to the congregation and community. Clergy, no less than other professional leaders, need to set boundaries about what to share about their personal lives in their professional settings. For example, a clergyperson who is thinking about divorcing his wife could not appropriately share that information with anyone in the parish without switching roles with the parishioner—the pastor using the parishioner as his or her confidant, instead of the reverse. Clergy have a right and an ethical responsibility to maintain privacy about issues they are working through with counseling help or about issues that have no direct impact on the congregation.

The difficulty with professional boundaries regarding personal information comes when a clergyperson has made a decision about divorce and needs to begin informing the congregation. Since a divorce may involve housing or relocation, salary issues, and changed relationships with people within the congregation, these issues do have a direct relationship to pastoral effectiveness during a time of transition. Initially (depending on the polity of the congregation), the chairperson of the governing board should be informed and limited information made available. Then the personnel committee is told, next the full board, and eventually the entire congregation.

As the circle of people in the know widens, clergy still have a right to determine how much info they will share with each group. When guarding privacy, clergy can slip into secret keeping when they hide information that has a direct bearing on the effectiveness of their work, their agreements with the congregation, or other significant relationships. When making disclosure decisions, clergy should consider what direct bearing their information has on individuals and the overall congregation.

As clergy discern what to conceal, what to reveal, and to whom, shame influences their decisions. Like all of us, clergy keep secrets about aspects of their lives that are deemed by them or others to be unacceptable. Clergy may damage their own well-being as well as their congregation's if they protect information about their personal shortcomings, self-questioning, theological beliefs, and sexual life out of fear or shame. Rather than protecting their privacy, they are keeping secrets.

The realm of sexual activity is particularly challenging. Congregations often pressure clergy to keep secrets about an especially key area of their lives—the significance of their relationships, if they are homosexual, or if they are single and choose to be sexually active—on threat of losing their ministerial standing. Congregations across the nation are trying to decide whether or not single clergy have the right to privacy when they are sexually active. Many denominations have ordination agreements that prohibit sexual relationships prior to, or outside of, heterosexual marriage. Religious officials may insist on knowing what a clergyperson considers absolutely private.

Some of the secrets clergy keep about themselves relate to physical or emotional functioning. While people of faith claim that their organizations are more accepting of physical and emotional illnesses than business workplaces, too few congregations welcome the full participation of clergy with disabilities. Candidates for ordination whose diseases could progress and might add to a congregation's cost for benefits may keep their condition secret lest it limit their future. To remain in the pulpit, pastors may keep secret the fact that they have become depressed, addicted, or anxious to the point that medication and mental health treatment is necessary. To exacerbate this tendency to hide their problems, clergy in congregations do not have the legal protections granted to employees in other settings, such as the Americans with Disabilities Act guidelines protecting disabled employees.

Clergy struggling with emotional issues may mistakenly presume, "No one will know if I don't tell anyone about it." Yet parishioners notice the changes in affect and functioning and can become highly critical about the ways that "our pastor has changed." Criticism simply adds to the malaise of the clergyperson as well as to isolation and job burnout. One secret may lead to other secrets, including personal and sexual boundary violations, resignations, and possibly even to suicide.

Secrets about Theology

Theological secrets are among the most difficult for clergy to address because they involve personal integrity and belief. At midcareer, pastors may feel great malaise or feel that their faith is no longer vital—but never speak about their spiritual lethargy. What if Sandra loses touch with God? What if Ron feels that he no longer believes in monotheism? What if Mike feels drawn to a sabbatical year of studying Buddhism or Islam? Perhaps Salina feels that the virgin birth is simply allegory and wonders whether or not it makes any difference. Sometimes clergy feel like imposters in the pulpit, because they have doubts about aspects of theology they are sure their parishioners think are at the heart of the faith.

Others avoid speaking at all about areas of controversy. To have to keep preaching the old story in the same old way is one of the most soul-wrenching experiences for clergy.

Most denominations have few mechanisms in place to address a clergyperson's theological disconnection from the parish. Clergy keep silent about deepening theological doubts or the sense that their personal beliefs have moved beyond the mainstream beliefs of their parishioners. Clergy may publicly present a "false self." This false self is maintained at a high cost to the emotional and psychological well-being of clergy. The resulting anxiety and doubt can often be growth producing, *if* the clergyperson has the freedom to explore and change. However, he or she may be limited by a fearful congregation or by personal fear about what might happen if controversial beliefs are fully disclosed. When a clergyperson is no longer a match with the congregation and does nothing to move on, the gap between the real self and the false self grows wider. Eventually the stress of trying to bridge this widening gap affects the physical and mental health of the clergyperson and the functioning of the congregation. Clergy who regularly bend or stretch their own "truths" to fit the needs of their congregations damage their own souls and the souls of others.

Instead of anxiously holding these doubts privately, clergy may relieve some tension by sharing their doubts with others. Attending a class or workshop might give clergy a chance to explore new scholarship and to share some of their less conventional ideas with colleagues. When doubts become overwhelming, spiritual direction or counseling is also an option that reduces the "imposter syndrome" and helps clergy privately process the personal secrets that are crippling them. Secret thoughts and feelings, if significant in number and in the degree of anxiety they produce, may also lead clergy to review their vocational fit and perhaps seek new directions in ministry. Denominational committees on ministry have begun to offer more pastoral options for career evaluation and discernment, knowing that clergy who are disconnected from themselves and others by secrecy will not function well and may damage congregations.

Secrets about Burnout and Addictions

Burnout is often a secret that clergy keep to themselves—or from themselves. This includes exhaustion, sleeplessness, increasingly addictive behavior, and a sense of hopelessness or anxiety. Burnout can lead to workaholism and other addictions because the physical body is depleted and seeks the high of new experience. A rush of adrenaline can be achieved by a win, by a risk-taking behavior, or by engaging in a taboo behavior. When the high wears off, the low and the accompanying shame lead to the desire to grab for the high again. Once repetitive behavior is engaged in, the anticipation of the high rises and the cycle repeats.

Growing numbers of clergy are becoming addicted to computer gambling and pornography. Computer addictions, whether playing games, blogging, or searching X-rated sites, are fueled by an online industry that knows the power of the hook and the behavioral changes that result from regular use. Clergy-kept secrets about addictions may or may not mask secrets about burnout or depression. Crossing boundaries may result from a physiological and psychological need to feel alive, vital, creative, and charming rather than depleted, hopeless, stifled, and old.

The way out of an addiction is through truthfulness, because secrets and shame underlie compulsive behavior. The family or individual shame of having to admit excessive alcohol use, for example, keeps the user from exposing the truth. If the addiction is seen as a moral issue, the participant feels even more hopeless and unworthy in the sight of God. Yet viewed through the perspective of a disease model, most addictions can be understood as behaviors that can be overcome rather than as a moral failing.

A congregation can support its members or staff who are committed to ending addictive behaviors, but only if those behaviors

become known. The addicted individual, the person's family, and
the congregation must acknowledge the reality of the addiction.
In letters sent to colleagues and members of his congregation, one
pastor courageously admitted his alcoholism and recovery effort
and gained his church's supportive encouragement for his recovery.
Once his secret couldn't be put back in the bottle, other members
of the congregation were inspired by his honesty and began to deal
with their own brokenness and addictions.

Secrets about Sexuality

Clergy in most denominations keep secrets about sexual orientation,
fidelity, and celibacy. Single clergy who date or engage in sexual
activity also keep this information to themselves. They have to or
their ordination could be at stake. The results of keeping one's sexual
orientation or interests private are subtle and can be devastating.
When someone is out of integrity internally (that is, carefully trying to present oneself as the same as others while knowing oneself
to be unique), it affects interpersonal integrity too.

In congregations with gay, lesbian, or bisexual clergy, many people are curious about their single clergyperson's romantic prospects.
Singles who are straight are often rumored to be gay or lesbian.
Gay and lesbian clergy with partners may be in a constant state
of having to hide the very relationship that married heterosexuals
celebrate quite publicly. Every conversation is affected. What do
you tell the staff about your vacation if you traveled with a sexual
partner to whom you are not married? Do you take the picture of
you and your partner off of the mantel when parishioners come to
visit?

The constant management of information to shield the truth is
extremely anxiety producing and exhausting. While the congregation experiences feelings of confusion and anxiety, as if "something's
not quite right here," the pastor is busily trying to reassure everyone
that things are fine. Clergy suffer from the delusion that they can
keep their sexual interest or orientation private in the congrega-

tional family without the erosion of personal and congregational vitality. People cannot live for long without congruency between words and actions, between the outside presentation and inner knowledge. Otherwise creative and effective clergy become limited in their freedom to fully embrace passion in their personal or professional lives—and their congregations also suffer from clergy secrecy.

Secrets about Family Issues

Janet's ordination followed the delivery of her first child by only a month. As church members gushed over the new baby, they also passed along stories of the senior pastor's adolescent daughter who had just run off with an ex-con. Unaware of the impact of their gossip on the new mom, several exclaimed that "clergy kids are always disasters." The fishbowl for clergy (mentioned in chapter 1) quickly turns normal family challenges into secrets. Troubled children, divorce, and other family dramas are difficult enough for parishioners but can become public nightmares for clergy. So personal life can easily go underground, splitting a clergyperson into two realms: a secret life as struggling parent and partner and the public life as polished pastor.

To protect her image as an effective pastor, Janet mastered the ability to hide any flaw or difficulty in her parenting and marriage from her congregation. No one knew how concerned she was about her children skipping school or their drug use. Later her divorce came as a major shock to others because her marital struggles had been such secrets. Shame about the disparity between her real life as a parent and wife and the perfect pastor life she thought was expected of her increased her secrecy and isolation. When the truth about her family life was revealed, she realized how much her secrecy had cost her in authenticity.

Janet realized that dynamics in her family of origin fueled her need to appear perfect; her mother needed to be perfect and so had kept much of her own life secret. In *The Secret Life of Families*, Evan Imber-Black writes, "A secret may be silently and unknowingly passed from generation to generation, like a booby-trapped heir-loom."[3] When clergy are hired or appointed to the congregations they grew up in, the legacy of family dynamics is exacerbated. One minister ended his clergy career because of his profound disempowerment by his congregation, which he said "always saw me as the little kid they once knew" and never as the pastor.

Clergy kids who grow up to become clergy themselves some-times struggle with a painful drive to replicate a ministry they observed in childhood. They may strive to become professionally important in the midst of profound self-doubt and comparison to a clergy parent, relative, or even the pastor of their childhood memories. An agenda of dogged determination to prove to a clergy parent or someone else that the now-ordained child can be a successful minister in his or her own right can create secrets. Old family of origin issues may continue to haunt and push them. All the while the secret that develops within the clergyperson, and often the whole congregation, is that the pastor is driven to win his father's approval or trying to make her mentor proud of her. Rather than serving the church without a personal agenda, these clergy carry the burden of the sometimes unrealistic expectations of parishioners combined with daunting inner expectations.

Overcoming Secrets

Secrets in congregations are inevitable. Some secrets result when positive intentions become distorted, as in the donor who fully funded the associate's salary. Some secrets are actually private infor-mation belonging to someone who has chosen to limit discussion, and this person's choice not to share the story should be respected unless there has been actual harm or there is a reasonable threat of harm contained in the information. Secrets arising from embar-rassing situations are more difficult to bring to light because of all their accompanying shame. However, when secrets are uncovered in a congregation, the energy that had been used to protect them can then be redirected toward healthy ministry.

Secrets may be commonplace but when faith leaders bump into them, the personal anxiety and angst within the congregation can be extremely uncomfortable. The layers of shame and secrecy created by addictions, sexual issues, and unethical practices in ministry can become especially toxic in congregations. To discharge those feelings and return to equilibrium and faith, leaders may be tempted to seal the secret up once more. The damage of those secrets will likely lead to others and inhibit leadership in the congregation for years to come. Secrets have no positive function in the life of the congregation. However, once a secret is disclosed it cannot really be concealed again. At that point, open discussion must take place with respect, humility, and forthrightness.

Chapter 3

Consequences of Secrets in Congregations

Beneath many a declining congregation lie one or more secrets that have harmed the community to the point of destruction. When congregations are barely maintaining the status quo or find themselves in a pattern of decline, they most likely are avoiding one or more painful secrets. For growth and vitality, secrets must be addressed. Congregational secrets have a wide range of consequences for communities of faith. Left unattended they will:

- limit interpersonal effectiveness
- compromise communication
- damage interpersonal relationships
- recruit other secret keepers
- inhibit playfulness and spontaneity
- distort power
- distract from mission and growth
- damage effective governance and leadership
- discourage healthy boundaries
- create anxiety and depression among clergy and leaders
- limit growth
- lead to congregational decline

Secrets Limit Personal Effectiveness

People with personal secrets find themselves spending a good deal of energy trying to protect their secrets from disclosure. Hiding a secret with shame attached to it becomes especially exhausting. Frequently, a secret keeper puts up a false front of acceptability and holiness while protecting any aspects of self that are believed to be flawed or unacceptable to others. Although this false front helps cover the secret, the person loses personal integrity and suffers from internal splitting. While everyone has a social self and a private self, an individual's mask of self-righteousness on the outside may shield an ashamed, carefully hidden person on the inside, a person no one really knows because that person has split off from his or her own truths.

Leaders with secrets often wonder, "What if they knew who I really am or what I have done?" These self-focused concerns occupy the mind of the secret keepers and diminish their capacity to relate to themselves, others, and God. Secrets may cover deeply held feelings of unworthiness and low self-esteem that limit the capacity for the authenticity essential for effective leadership. Relational intimacy requires appropriate personal disclosure, and secret keeping inhibits that disclosure. Without this intimacy, leadership takes place in a vacuum devoid of spiritual vitality.

Secrets Compromise Communication

Secrets compromise communication by limiting what can be discussed. If a family with an adopted child decides not to tell the child she is adopted, communication becomes distorted to protect the secret. What may be talked about, when, and by whom? Some questions about the past are evaded. Communication strategies are developed to distract attention from the hidden truth, often one that is already known and simply not discussed. If part of the adoption secret is that the birth mother is the sister of the adoptive mother, an even broader circle of communication distortion takes place. In such cases, people in the broader system not only don't talk about the adoption but they also avoid talking about the aunt, the aunt's life story, the father of the child, or the resemblance of the child to other family members. For no reason apparent to those who don't know the secret, unacceptable questions are dodged in conversations. The child may look at a family photo album of the aunt and her own father and never know that these are her birth parents. If she asks, "Who are these people?" she may be told, "Put away the book, and don't ask so many questions." Or an out-and-out lie may be told to cover up the truth.

Not only the secret subject but other subjects that might lead the conversation closer to the secret are avoided. Let's say a pastor's alcoholism is a secret in a parish. To protect this secret, those who know the secret only associate with other individuals who know it. Those who don't know are left out of communication with those who do. Alliances form and divisions take place. As Rabbi Edwin H. Friedman wrote in his foundational work *Generation to Generation*, "Secrets function to divide a family, as an avalanche would a community. Those 'in' on the secret will become far better able to communicate with one another than with those in the outsider group, about any issue, not just about the secret."[1]

The secret interferes with direct and open communication, especially the expression of feelings and opinions, and the secret keeping involves pretense, deceit, or evasion on a daily basis. Friedman offers the example of a minister visiting a family in the waiting room of an intensive care unit. The minister had been notified of the brother's death, but when he talked with family members, he immediately realized that none of them had been told of the death. He wondered why doctors hadn't said anything, so he thought he shouldn't either. "He spent so much time pre-thinking everything he said, for fear it would lead to questions about the brother, that he was totally unable to be the spontaneous self that was the basis of his pastoral effectiveness."[2]

Secrecy places those in the know in a conflict between protecting and exposing the secret. Most families and most congregational families adopt tacit "don't ask, don't tell" policies, particularly regarding secrets about sexuality or other issues that evoke shame. When asking questions or telling is not okay, communication within the congregation becomes limited by distorted perceptions, misconceptions, and a lack of factual information. For example, when a lay leader stopped by the church one evening, he heard the pastor swearing and was alarmed. He observed through the office window that the pastor was engaged in online gambling. Not sure what to do with the information, the leader was caught between his loyalty to the pastor, eagerness to protect the image of congregation, and a real desire to share this information with certain people who could help the pastor address this behavior. Because this was a congregation that rarely talked about anything that wasn't "nice," he felt he could do nothing but pray privately and hope that it was a one-time incident. In a congregation open where transparency and direct feedback are the norm, he would have known whom to tell and have had confidence that his telling wouldn't backfire.

Secrets Damage Interpersonal Relationships

In congregations where truths are hidden or distorted, people become anxious and hypervigilant. They intuitively sense that it's not a safe environment. Authentic interpersonal relationships and community depend on trust, honesty, and connection—and are damaged by distrust, dishonesty, evasion, and divisiveness. Secrets affects not only those who consciously withhold the information but also the entire congregation.

Congregational secrets lead to insider-outsider dynamics. Those insiders who know the real story align with others in the know and exclude those who don't know. New people in a congregation may not be told the full history of the congregation because the pastor and lay leaders paint a rosy picture to recruit new members. New people who find their way into leadership positions may feel like they are in the dark most of the time. New clergy may be unable to claim their authority. Relationships lack integrity and intimacy. Therefore new members have superficial relationships with the old timers who protect the secret. Without experiencing authentic connection to others, they may soon leave the congregation. Authentic relationship demands a level of intimacy that cannot be achieved without exposing the truth.

Secrets Recruit Secret Keepers

An insidious result of a secret-keeping congregation is that it attracts individuals who have damaging secrets in their own lives. The person with sexual shame is drawn to a congregation with unresolved sexuality issues. The person with a rejected homosexual family member is drawn to a congregation that keeps its gay and lesbian leaders "in the closet." A person with a gambling addiction feels at home in a congregation where the pastor's addiction has gone undisclosed.

When the secret is about the pastor, priest, or rabbi of a congregation or a religious order, great damage results. Members tend to play follow the leader and keep secrets too. Distortions of information especially abound in congregations where the clergyperson is engaged in secret keeping about sexual partnerships. Everyone in the congregation may actually know, though they have not been specifically told. This unspoken truth, or even speculation, distorts every relationship within the congregation and every person consciously or unconsciously colludes with the secret keeping by not asking or not telling. Other devastating results of secrecy overtake the congregation. Insider-outsider dynamics take place, new members find themselves confused and disoriented, and subsequent leaders are not trusted.

Secrets Inhibit Playfulness and Spontaneity

Whole congregations can become depressed because the energy that fuels spiritual vitality is absorbed in protecting the secret. Symptoms of a depressed congregation include the following:

- a loss of playfulness and spontaneity
- a loss of childlike wonder and spiritual aliveness
- an increasing frustration and codependency on the part of clergy and lay leaders

When people act with spontaneity and playfulness, they drop their defenses and relax, thereby increasing pleasure and trust. Individuals and congregations with secrets lose this characteristic due to fear that if they relax they might let information slip. New ideas become threatening, change is inhibited, humor becomes sarcasm, and the spiritual vitality of the congregation declines from lack of joy and authentic fun. Also, the lack of pleasure in things that had once brought joy signals burnout—and burnout sets the stage for boundary crossings.

Secrets Distort Power

When a pastor began using language that the office staff deemed to border on harassment, the office manager, Judy, decided to tell the congregation's personnel committee. Her meeting with the chairperson seemed to go well. She was satisfied that he said he would speak to the pastor and would inform the committee about her concern. However, six months later the pattern of communication hadn't stopped; the pastor continued to use language Judy had asked him to never use in her presence or around other women in the parish. So she asked a member of the personnel committee if anything had ever been mentioned to the committee about some of the pastor's harassing comments. The member looked puzzled. "I've been to all of the meetings, Judy, and I can't tell you exactly what we talk about in detail, but that subject has never come up."

Judy was hurt and felt discounted. The personnel committee chairperson had the responsibility and the power to end the hostile work environment but instead intentionally chose to conceal the information about the pastor's behavior from the committee. His secret keeping manipulated the situation and left Judy and other women exposed to the pastor's abusive language. She was furious. She was angry at the pastor and at the whole church for not taking seriously her need for a safe and respectful work environment. The lack of integrity within the organization was deeply painful to her. She began to withdraw from her friends, coworkers, and eventually sought other employment. The chairperson's choice to keep the allegations quiet led to a series of broken relationships.

Those who know something have more power than those who do not, whether the information is vital to the life of the congregation or seemingly less crucial. Over lunch at a workshop, a congregation's new education director overheard the pastor talking about a former pastor's sexual relationship with her predecessor. "What?" exclaimed the new director, who was sitting at the table, "I didn't know that!" When the pastor responded, "Well, everybody knows it," she was disappointed to have begun her ministry without such a key piece of information. It accounted for the erratic, exaggerated, and unexplainable comments and reactions toward her the past few months. If "everybody knows" something, anyone left out of the "everybody" lacks the information necessary to make sense of his or her own situation and may be set up to flounder in a cluelessness that reduces effectiveness of his or her leadership or ministry.

Secrets Distract from Mission and Growth

Oftentimes families and faith leaders change the subject in conversation or behave strangely to hide a less than favorable truth.

Distraction protects secrets. A church with internal financial problems mounts a capital campaign. A congregation with an ineffective pastor develops a new lay ministry to compensate for the pastor's weakness. A synagogue dealing with an allegation of sexual misconduct focuses on reorganizing the board and committees.

Sometimes a congregation distracts from the secret by a new program or a new project. Externals become the center of congregational attention. The congregation fixes up the building—spending hundreds of thousands of dollars to look good on the outside—while worship attendance drops. Rather than address internal shame over the secret or tell the truth about the secrets in the congregation's past, members spruce up the outside and hope that this veneer suffices.

Protecting a secret requires immense emotional energy that could better be focused on mission and growth in the congregation. The more faith leaders feel themselves or the congregation to be threatened, the more likely they are to distract from, rather than fulfill, the core mission of the congregation.

Secrets Lead to Distrust in Leadership

Several years after a pastor had been removed from ministry due to sexual misconduct, the congregation he had served showed numerous signs of the decline, including decreased worship attendance, few new members, a negative image of the congregation in the community, and a palpable malaise among congregational leaders. The most telling result of the damage was that the current pastor wasn't being allowed to lead the congregation. His ideas were rejected, his well-formed sermons were described as lacking in integrity, and he was outvoted at every meeting. The current pastor assumed that everyone knew the story of his predecessor's misconduct, the problems had been resolved, and the congregation had moved on. But in reality, the leaders had never gathered together to share how the misconduct had affected them, what they felt about it, and how it rocked their faith. Neither the pastor nor the congregation had connected the congregation's lack of trust for its new pastor to the earlier pastor's secret sexual relationship. Deep in the minds and spirits of congregation members issues were not resolved, and the resultant mistrust of all pastoral leadership limited congregational vitality. Without trust from the congregation, the current pastor's role was extremely limited. However, trust could be rebuilt with a thorough review of the damage from prior pastoral secrets and a pledge to be transparent in the future.

Congregational mistrust can lead to a decline in membership and vitality. When a problem is covered up or minimized as no big deal, injured parties express frustration and become vocal about the systemic cover up or leave the congregation. Not only are current leaders then suspect but future leaders will have to earn back the trust of the congregation. When congregational leaders started a preschool at First Church in Concord, they put a lot of personal time and effort into the project. Once the school was up and running, they became less involved and eventually stopped going to the board meetings of their own preschool—that is until the pastor opened the mail to find a letter from the Internal Revenue Service saying that a significant amount of past taxes, related to the operation of the school, were due. A subsequent investigation led to the allegation that the preschool director had embezzled large sums of money and, as a result, payroll taxes had not been paid. As the director's secrets became public knowledge, the board corrected the situation with as much openness as possible.

The trust of a congregation in its leaders declines whenever a secret is exposed, but had the board learned of the situation and tried to cover it up, the consequences would have been far worse. This congregation understood that covering up secrets, even old ones, leads to mistrust in the organization, in the integrity of its leaders, and in the institution as a steward of God's bounty. The leaders of First Church handled the situation with full openness within the congregation and community, raising trust in their leadership and gaining the financial support of members to repay the debt.

Secrets Discourage Healthy Boundaries

Two possible extremes develop in congregations that have lived with secrets. Congregations either create overly rigid patterns of congregational interaction and approaches to problems, or congregations are so laissez-faire that boundaries about behavior and expectations are unclear or nonexistent. Either extreme damages congregational functioning.

Rigid boundaries develop to protect the secret with tacit but strict rules about communication, "how things are done around here," and who can do what. Leaders are swift to pronounce judgment on those who break the code of silence about particular topics. Invisible brick walls seem to replace the healthier, negotiable boundaries that define what is appropriate and inappropriate. Poor boundaries can even encourage secret-keeping dynamics when no secret exists!

Laissez-faire leadership styles may hide a secret in confusion and chaos. No one really may know what information is accurate, who to trust, who is accountable to whom, or what is going on. The lackadaisical, look-the-other-way attitude and cheap grace abound such that leaders can do almost anything without question or accountability. With such fluid boundaries, individuals feel confused about their roles, become enmeshed from lack of guidelines, and appear to be in a group trance, unable to see the dysfunction of the congregational culture.

One pastor chose to preach only twice a month, though she was hired because of her special gift for preaching, and she rarely appeared at congregational gatherings or even in her office. No one seemed to know where she was or how to get in touch with her. The congregation rambled along in a fog of disarray because they had become used to secrets in that church's history. Often in a family with secrets, a family member will say, "I'm always confused." In a congregation with secrets, members will also stay confused. Nothing and no one seems reliable. Without trust and clarity of direction, a congregation, over time, tends to lose a sense of its true purpose.

Secrets Create Anxiety and Depression

Secret keeping both creates and feeds on intense emotional anxiety. People who keep secrets suppose they are protecting themselves and others from the anxiety of disclosure, but the reverse is true. When Pastor Cherie began to feel attracted to a leader in her church, she knew that she could not cross sexual boundaries with him, even though both of them were single. As a clergywoman, she had been trained in clergy ethics and understood that because of her role, she was the person with greater power in a relationship with a congregant and that to express her romantic desires in any way would leave him with more than flattery. He would possibly lose his source of pastoral care, and to date her he might have to leave the congregation. Or if dating went awry, he might complain to denominational authorities about her misuse of position and power.

Cherie fought against her own desires to get to know the man more closely; she tried to be around him only when others were present and to go on about church business as if nothing was happening. The problem was that she invested so much of her energy into containment of her secret interest in the man. Since he was off limits to her, she became more tense and anxious about her desires. She distracted herself with meaningless tasks, lost interest in her own work, resented her call to ministry, and became sullen and withdrawn. As her self-image lowered, her self-focus and isolation increased. Carrying a lonely secret made her a less effective clergy leader. People around her sensed her anxiety and, having no understanding of its source, backed away from her. Without the light-hearted approach she usually took toward ministry, the entire congregation began to feel heavy and depressed. Until she took her secret attraction to a safe church consultant to explore, she was ineffective in leadership. Had she not done this, the congregation itself would have declined in vitality.

Consequences of Clergy-Kept Secrets

To hold a secret and be a person of integrity is very difficult. In his book *Stigma: Notes on the Management of Spoiled Identity*, social psychologist Erving Goffman aptly describes the dilemma of a clergyperson with a secret. Every action, every communication is internally monitored by the individual with the secret: "To display or not to display; to tell or not to tell; to let on or not to let on; to lie or not to lie; and in each case, to whom, how, when and where."[3] This internal hypervigilance is psychically exhausting.

The burden of carrying a secret in one's own soul eventually isolates clergy. Secrets are often at the core of obsessive and compulsive behaviors. They lead to intractable attitudes and crossing interpersonal boundaries. As clergy keep secrets that they believe would discredit them, they also limit their social intimacy. Clergy with secrets function at a distance from others that replicates the distance and disconnection within themselves. How clergy manage information can alter and distort their life story. The phrase "in the closet" aptly describes the darkness of the spirit that encroaches upon those who are culturally stigmatized yet try to keep up the pretense of being something they are not—whether that is celibate, straight, theologically congruent, perfect, and so on.

Consequences of Clergy Secrets

Clergy may act out by

- manipulating others and facts to protect the secret
- abusing power and position
- increasing obsessive or addictive behavior

- failing to practice good self-care
- damaging interpersonal relationships, especially intimate ones
- becoming workaholic in an effort to escape or prove oneself
- fostering more secrets or protected information

Clergy may suffer internally from

- self-deception and limited self-awareness
- shame and guilt over the protected information
- isolation to reduce the chance of someone discovering the secret
- denial, minimization, and rationalization related to the secret
- repression of emotions and depression
- erosion of conscience (inability to determine right or wrong)
- splitting and development of false self

Congregations may be confused about

- why the pastor is distant, depressed, distracted, or not what he or she used to be
- why the clergyperson's spouse or partner is absent, hidden, sullen, relationally cold
- why congregants have so many questions and feel so uncomfortable

---

Secrets Lead to Congregational Decline

Church consultant Kenneth Mitchell notes, "There is hardly anything so powerfully destructive in a system as the shutting down of communication or the development and maintenance of secrets."[4] The dangers of congregational secrets are so great that the congregation can fall into a pattern of decline and eventually close its doors. Leaders struggling to keep a secret create illusions, distort information, and concoct a version of history that leaves out pertinent data. When fearful of disclosure and always looking around for sources of threat, they become increasingly anxious. If more key leaders keep up the deception, others become confused and mystified and are manipulated into collusion. And secrets beget other secrets. Congregational growth becomes difficult as trust in leaders erodes and all of the leaders' and members' emotional resources are invested in maintaining the secret.

When congregational clergy or leaders carry organizational secrets, they end up with interpersonal and intrapersonal burdens as well. The complexity multiplies. The interactions between them become distorted with a blurring of boundaries or with rigid boundaries. Shame replaces grace. People in congregations with secrets either look everywhere with scrutiny or simply look the other way. Ultimately, the secrecy distorts self-perception as well as perceptions about others, the congregation, and God. When passion for life, for God, and for ministry decline, the congregation itself is at risk. If secrecy continues to fester, stagnation and decline lead to chronic dysfunction and eventually congregational demise. While the congregation's exterior presentation may look good for a while, the facade crumbles and collapses in on itself.

Yet secrets can be opened and their negative consequences reversed. A congregation that strives to be safe and transparent, where old secrets are opened and handled with care and honesty, can recreate itself. Where leaders and clergy seek the truth and speak the truth in love, growth and change lead to new and inspiring ministry.

Chapter 4

Disclosure:
Patterns and Consequences

Withholding information that people need to know clearly damages the health of a congregation and its leaders. The reverse dynamic also cripples congregational life. Disclosing information that is inappropriate, inaccurate, or uncontrolled is common in any group. In faith communities, out-of-bounds communication thrives because most information is revealed orally and informally and is easily transmitted without limits. People want to know what is going on in the life of the congregation and its members. When information is withheld or missing, the void fills with rumors and gossip. Appropriate channels of communication and sources of accurate information may be disregarded. People enjoy the power of knowing information that other people lack, so they sometimes share stories even if they had formally agreed to protect the information. Members of personnel or pastoral search committees may tell their spouses or partners information that should be protected. Clergy may accidentally or intentionally reveal the personal stories of a congregant. Disclosing too much can be as problematic as concealing too much. The World War II slogan "loose lips sink ships" applies to congregational boats as well.

Four Problematic Types of
Revealed Information

The release of information becomes problematic when formal or social boundaries are ignored or when the information revealed is inaccurate. *Rumors* are misinformation that is fabricated in the absence of accurate information. For example, when no one knew why Pastor Lombera didn't show up to lead worship, explanatory rumors began to circulate instantly based on nothing but speculation. Information contained in *gossip* may be more accurate but becomes problematic because it is spread outside formal informational channels. The congregation's president announced that Pastor Lombera was absent due to illness, but a church member saw him drinking late the night before at a party and eagerly gossiped to others, as if factual, that the pastor had a bad hangover.

Sometimes too much information, more than is customary or acceptable by social norms, is revealed. *Exposure* is sharing personal data that would normally be reserved for a more intimate or confidential relationship. Pastor Lombera became alarmed at the rumors and gossip circulating about his absence, and during his pastoral message the next Sunday rambled on about struggles with his wife and how a fight with her had kept him from getting to church the week before. He exposed private information about his marital relationship in the public setting of worship. Not only was his wife horrified, but everyone at the service was disturbed to hear so much detail.

The last problematic type of revealed information is *leaking*, when information is released in spite of relevant and agreed upon boundaries to keep it contained. The personnel committee gathered to determine how to deal with the escalating anxiety caused by the pastor's absence, the subsequent rumors and gossip, and the pastor's inappropriate open discussion of his family problems. When meeting with Pastor Lombera, the committee learned that he had a drinking problem and decided to grant him a two-week leave to begin recovery. The committee's decision was to be announced at the next council meeting, but ignoring the agreement to protect the information until the meeting, one of the personnel committee members leaked the information over coffee with another church member.

These four troublesome communication styles—rumors, gossip, exposure, and leaking—will each be explored more thoroughly in the following sections.

Rumors

The most widely cited psychological theory of rumor defines rumor as "a specific (or topical) proposition for belief, passed along from person to person, usually by word of mouth, without secure standards of evidence being present."[1] In other words, rumors are not based on accurate information but are constructed around speculation or unauthenticated information, and therefore are pseudo-information. A rumor has no standard evidence, cannot be verified, and may even be deliberate misinformation.

One congregation was distraught that both the associate pastor and senior pastor divorced within months of one another, and members longed for explanations. Because the divorces were personal tragedies, neither pastor discussed specifics with their parishioners. In most work settings, this amount of privacy about such personal information would be appropriate. However, congregations often want, and sometimes receive, more detailed personal revelation. When members expect to know more about their clergy but don't, they tend to fill in the gap. In an information void, speculation abounds. Though the two divorces were totally unrelated and the two pastors not the least bit socially (much less romantically) interested in one another, the situation was ripe with curiosity and speculation. During this time of upheaval, the senior pastor asked to borrow the associate pastor's mountain cabin for a father-son weekend. The next Tuesday in the church's reception area, he handed the associate pastor the cabin's laundered towels and sheets with keys on top, thanking her profusely for the wonderful weekend. "We'll have to do that again," he glowed. "It meant so much to me." The volunteer who answered the phones watched with delight, eager to tell the others at the Women's Fellowship luncheon that day what she had witnessed. By afternoon word had spread that the two pastors were having an affair.

Causes of Rumors

Seeds of rumor are planted when evidence pertaining to an important topic is ambiguous, concealed, or otherwise unavailable. When normal channels of communication break down, people seek alternate means of obtaining information and theorize on their own and with acquaintances to try to explain a confusing situation. We all are motivated to make sense of our environment and to understand our circumstances. So we seek explanations or meanings to reduce or eliminate chaos and uncertainty and to reconcile dissonant beliefs. Psychologists and researchers Ralph Rosnow and Gary Fine explain, "When the truth is not directly forthcoming we piece together information as best we can, giving rise to rumors, rationalizations, and the search for a definition of the situation. The reason rumors circulate is that they explain things and relieve the tensions of uncertainty."[2] Rumors are an attempt to provide structure in an uncertain situation, bring a sense of closure, and simplify complex situations. No wonder rumors are so common.

When an associate pastor was suddenly terminated without a stated reason, the congregation was shocked and saddened. Members were given no information upon which to understand the pastor's dismissal. A few hints circulated that the associate and senior pastor had personality differences, but this hardly seemed significant enough to warrant sudden dismissal. With so little information, rumors began to circulate that the associate had resigned due to a critical physical illness. While this was not the case, it caused enough damage to the associate's reputation that finding another job became difficult.

In addition to providing explanations, rumors provide an outlet for anxieties and hostilities. Instead of acknowledging these uncomfortable feelings, someone deals with them indirectly and creates a rumor to express his or her anxiety, anger, or frustration. One of the first psychologists to study personality, Gordon Allport, wrote, "In reality [a rumor's] hidden expressive functions are more important than its alleged informative functions."[3] Rather than being received as a reliable mode of discourse and authentically informative, rumors should be taken as disclosing more about the one who tells it than about the situation the teller describes.[4]

However, rumors are often taken as reliable information rather than being heard as opinions, venting, or a method for coping with high anxiety. For example, rumors often percolate around financial issues in a congregation. Even when the endowment held millions of dollars and the general fund continued to increase annually, an East Coast congregation continued to believe rumors that funds were short and staff would be laid off. Those rumors actually related to anxiety about the pending retirement of the senior rabbi, a topic sealed from public discussion, and not concern about the congregation's financial health at all.

Rumors are particularly rampant during or after a crisis, disaster, or exciting or mysterious event that has not been fully explained. A combination of fear, confusion, and high anxiety, in addition to a dearth of information, fuels the rumors—like the famous rumor that a tidal wave swallowed New York City at the same time the earthquake hit San Francisco in 1906.[5] That a flurry of rumors followed immediately after announcements of the World Trade Center disaster on September 11, 2001, is understandable. In a crisis our usual psychological anchors may no longer be relevant or operational; our normal reference points by which we judge information crumble and our credulity stretches. Irrationality and distorted perceptions support the creation of rumors.[6] When a minister suddenly leaves under allegations of abuse, both the crisis and the necessary withholding of certain details fuel rumors that are often worse than the reality, or the reverse—rumors that downplay the seriousness of the situation.

In a congregational crisis, the insight and critical ability of a congregation often is suspended or reduced, and its vulnerability to rumormongering is especially high. The higher the anxiety, the more likely rumors will be fabricated. When the rector of a parish preached about his homosexual orientation, the anxiety level of his congregants rose to an all-time high. Although they had supported the election of a gay bishop and welcomed gay, lesbian, and bisexual members into the congregation, many members were unprepared to be led by a gay pastor. The congregation felt betrayed because members had not been told about his sexual orientation at the time of his hiring. Why hadn't he told them? Why hadn't the bishop told them? And what would it mean for them to have a gay pastor? The anxiety related to these questions precipitated a rumor by one spiteful parishioner that the pastor had been sexually seductive with him. He left the details vague and refused to file a formal complaint. Instead his insinuations and false rumors were sufficiently powerful to result in the termination of the pastor's relationship with the congregation.

In addition to providing a release for anxiety, rumors have another benefit for the speaker. As Allport explains, "To be 'in the know' exalts one's self-importance. While telling a tale a person is, for the time being, dominant over his listeners."[7] Studies of the differences between rumormongers and nonrumormongers have shown that rumormongers are less popular, date less often, and get together with friends less frequently. Spreading rumors may be an effort to gain self-esteem and social acceptance. The recipient of the rumor bestows status on the rumormonger merely by accepting what is said.[8]

Stories traveled rapidly around the community about a single female pastor who was planning to take a parishioner on her sabbatical trip overseas. The rumor was fueled by actual observations about how much time the two had spent together working on church issues. Each person passing on the rumor of romance enjoyed being in the know, especially if he or she could add another detail to the increasing elaborate story. Finally a clergy colleague was brave enough to confront the pastor, only to find out the parishioner's wife and child were also going on the trip. Though such a special relationship with one parishioner may not be appropriate, at least the rumors of a sabbatical affair were not true.

Given these motivations for creating and disseminating rumors, can one say that the social effects of rumors are all negative? In fact, rumors may be deleterious, beneficial, or indifferent.[9] As a specialist in rumors, Rosnow notes that a rumor "takes on whatever values are inherent in the situation."[10] When no other means of communication are possible or safe, rumors flourish. So the fact that rumors are being spread can give congregational leaders clues to possible problems.

- Do congregants not feel safe communicating directly and truthfully?
- Do rumors hint of high anxiety, negativity, or misuse of power?
- Do the rumors indicate that necessary information has been concealed?
- Do they indicate that a congregational member needs to be given more information, or perhaps less?
- Does the fact that someone is spreading rumors indicate the need for a pastoral response?
- Could the rumormonger's need for affirmation be eliminated if that individual received redirection and positive attention from congregational leaders?

When rumors about their church flew around town, copastors Sally and Juan wondered if they should have handled the dismissal of an ineffective education director differently. Several years into their ministry, the congregation's personnel committee had hired

Eva to help her out after her divorce and layoff from teaching at a local school. The committee had conscientiously taken steps to increase Eva's effectiveness as education director, but she became angry and refused to attend educational workshops or be coached by the pastors to build a more successful Sunday school program.

Sally and Juan finally realized that nothing short of Eva's dismissal would save the floundering program, and they fired her. Eva's friends in the parish rallied around her and refused to accept her dismissal. The pastors and personnel committee carefully explained that goals for the position had been clear, steps toward increasing effectiveness had proven unsuccessful, and while they valued her personally, Eva was no longer aligned with the mission and ministry of the congregation. But the logic of the dismissal didn't appease Eva or her friends. One particularly angry family bought an ad in the local paper criticizing the pastor's actions. By coincidence, a week later a gardener mowing the parsonage lawn hit a rock and a spark ignited the grass, which set fire to the garage. The rumor flew (and was believably received around town) that the parsonage had been purposely set ablaze.

The stronger the emotional reaction someone has to a rumor, the more likely they are to pass it on—even if they don't or can't believe it.[11] So the town was awash with grand stories of "the arson." To counteract this misinformation, the personnel committee and pastors spent much of their time correcting the story. But this rumor was the symptom of something more serious than a lack of information. Like other rumors, this one revealed deeper levels of anxiety and mistrust.

The presence and intensity of rumors prompt conscientious faith leaders to question communication patterns and the use of power and position within their congregation. Did Sally and Juan's congregants feel railroaded by a decision but not able to express themselves through legitimate channels? Were there seemingly unrelated, preexisting conflicts or anxiety among members? Wise leaders recognize rumors as symptoms of problems, then address dynamics within the congregation that need attention. As writer

Jessamyn West says of good fiction, a rumor can, for believers, "reveal a truth that reality obscures."

Challenges of Rumors

Rumors are common and problematic because they are inaccurate information and tend to spread easily. Rumors are unverified information and may even be deliberate misinformation. Researchers Allport and Postman explain the difficulty: "In rumor there is often some residual particle of news, as 'kernel of truth,' but in the course of transmission it has become so overlaid with fanciful elaboration that it is no longer separable or detectable."[12] The elaboration may be intentional or simply a result of personal filters dependent on the hearer and the spreader's predisposition. The teller is interpreting an incident within his or her larger frame of reference. It requires a good deal of insight to listen with the proper blend of appreciation and caution to a rumor.[13]

Rumormongering is a process of information dispersion as well as the product of that process. This informal process may be easier to start (and its product easier to disseminate) than to stop, because those who disseminate rumors ignore appropriate lines of communication. Congregational life can be profoundly affected by the spread of unverified, often inaccurate information. Two efforts may minimize rumors within a faith community: a communication road map and a rumor-control system.

A *communication road map* outlines the appropriate channels for finding out needed facts, expressing concerns, and relaying information. If you are worried about the safety of a child, whom do you talk to? If you are angry about the worship service running more than an hour, whom do you tell? These simple maps reflect the organizational or committee chart for the congregation. To be most effective they include procedures for handling concerns if the first contact person cannot resolve the issue. Whom do you talk to next?

For years Gladys, an experienced and devoted church secretary, watched young women dressed in halter tops and short skirts visit

the pastor. Each time one of them visited, the pastor would remind
Gladys that they did not want to be disturbed. She convinced herself
that she was just old-fashioned and judgmental, so kept quiet about
what she was witnessing. Everyone in the church seemed to adore
this pastor and the elected leadership gave him carte blanche, so
she thought that no one would believe her or take her concerns
seriously. Had there been a communication road map to direct her
to the pastoral relations committee, Gladys would have known how
to communicate her concerns instead of struggling alone. If the
pastoral relations committee was in the pastor's "back pocket," then
the map might have directed her to the church's governing body or
denominational leaders. Because Gladys was unable to proactively
address the situation via clear communication channels, addressing
the pastor's inappropriate activity required an intervention beyond
the local church. One of the young women finally filed a lawsuit
against the pastor for breach of fiduciary responsibility and only
then did his behavior stop.

What every congregation needs is *a rumor-control system*. During World War II, concern about the spread of misinformation led
the government to create a Rumor Project in the Office of War
Information.[14] As soon as misinformation was detected in the press
or in sidewalk conversations, official releases with the accurate
information were distributed to correct any misunderstandings,
reducing fear among the citizens at home and troops abroad.
Congregations could certainly adapt and benefit from regularly
and quickly rectifying erroneous information.

Correcting a rumor with accurate information works better than
trying to track a rumor's source. The informal spread of a rumor
makes determining its origin difficult, and the farther from the
source, the more inaccurate and complicated the rumor becomes.
Also, people tend to judge the credibility of a rumor by the reli-
ability of the person or source they hear it from, rather than by the
credibility of the original source.

Often anonymous people are added to the rumor to give it more
punch, like the rumor that "lots of people know that Jacob resigned
because of his drinking." Anyone in a congregation is familiar with

the phrases "They say . . ." or "Everyone thinks . . ." Congregational leaders often give too much credibility to anonymous groups (such as "they" and "everyone") and could help their congregations by stating that they will not take anonymous feedback seriously.

Similar to the problems with anonymous sources, material sent via e-mail to all recipients as blind copies makes it impossible to know who has the information, to control its dissemination to others, or for anyone to correct it if it is inaccurate. Rumormongering via blind e-mails is particularly insidious and must be immediately addressed. Leaders and congregants need to be urged to ignore e-mail, letters, and other communication from anonymous sources and to treat it like spam.

Finally, rumors are problematic because they divert attention and energy away from actual issues. In the earlier story about the gardener accidentally setting the parsonage's garage on fire, the rumor diverted from the real issue—the education director's performance and possibly other anxiety within the congregation. Instead of addressing the reality that the education director was inept, the congregation focused on rumors about who might have started the fire, even though the accurate information was easily available. Rumors deflect or distract attention from real problems a congregation may find too difficult to address directly.

Gossip

What congregation is free from gossip? Gossip, like rumor, is informal communication that can spread without control, usually orally. Unlike rumor, gossip has some basis in fact, though the significance of the facts is distorted and exaggerated by the teller and through many tellings. Whereas rumors usually deal with events and issues of great importance, gossip is trivial and nonessential, typically dealing with the personal affairs of individuals. Though gossip may serve a social purpose in enhancing relationship, it can also be arbitrary and mean-spirited. Gossip's greatest damage comes from its being a social exchange about other people who are absent (isolated or excluded) or treated as absent. Those who are gossiped about cannot speak for themselves or correct misinformation and thus become powerless, confused, and at worst paranoid about others' treatment of them, because they don't know what is being said about them.

Ironically, the origin of the word *gossip* relates to faith. In Middle English, the word was *godsibb*: *god* (god) + *sib* (kinsman), expressing our relationship to one another as children of God and therefore siblings. Although not used now, "godparent," "companion," or "a close friend" are other meanings of *gossip*. Reframing gossip as an exchange between "godsibbs," or siblings in God, would certainly transform its usual meaning as the chatty, trivial spreading of personal information and reduce the entertainment or titillation of sharing indiscreet talk about others.

Reasons for Gossip

Like rumors, gossip thrives where secrets hide or where needed information is absent. Author and psychologist William White warns that secret keeping "incites a frenzy of intelligence gathering that usually goes by the name 'gossip.' As the credibility of formal information channels declines, indigenous sources of information can wield enormous informal power in the organization."[15]

In one congregation, the volunteer responsible for sorting the congregation's mail noticed that Janice repeatedly sent letters marked "confidential" to the pastor. The flood of letters reminded the volunteer of the individuals who relentlessly called the county's suicide hotline, which he answered on Tuesdays. Those troubled individuals called often because they just needed someone to talk with. Unaware that this was a personnel issue and that Janice was chair of the personnel committee, the volunteer surmised that Janice suffered from mental instability and was begging the pastor for attention. For the volunteer, the repeated letters represented crisis—but he mistook a confidential personnel crisis for a personal crisis. Concerned about Janice, he asked his prayer partners to pray for her. Of course, the gossip about her many letters to the pastor sped throughout the congregation. No one checked with Janice personally, so the gossip continued. When the personnel issue had been resolved and the resulting decision could be shared with the congregation, congregants were embarrassed by their eagerness to spread speculation about the letters and their meaning.

Is gossip simply about filling a void of information? Evolutionary psychologists argue that gossip binds people and communities together. When gossip involves spending time with friends and sharing stories about mutual acquaintances, relationships are enhanced. Gossip provides networking, influence, and social alliances. In his research, psychologist Robin Dunbar found that 60 percent of human conversation is spent gossiping about relationships and personal experiences, much involving third parties not present.[16] However inevitable and blameless gossip may be, professor Nigel Nicholson says, "The problem with gossip lies in its content, which reflects precisely what is going on in people's minds."[17] He suggests the toxicity of the gossip mirrors the health of the organization. His model, translated for faith communities, implies that the healthier the congregation is, the closer its communication is to "godsibbing" than to gossiping.

Gossip is not merely idle talk, but talk with a social purpose. It helps people to learn the values and social etiquette of a group. A newcomer to a congregation soon learns how to behave by listening to the gossip during the coffee hour, in the parking lot, in prayer groups, and even in the pastoral prayers. One woman may be mocked behind her back for bringing her Bible to church. The listener decides never to bring hers. Gossip about members' children informs new parents about the congregation's expectations. One pastor overheard criticism of children's scuffed shoes at church and began to take time on Sunday morning before church to polish her baby's shoes.

Deborah Tannen explains this dynamic of gossip:

We measure our behavior against the potential for gossip, hearing in our minds how others are likely to talk about us. In trying to decide what to do, we automatically project contemplated actions onto the backdrop of this imagined dialogue, and our decisions about how to act are influenced by what we think others would say about them. Having decided, we hide, adjust or display our behavior to prevent criticism and ensure being praised. . . . [T]he assumptions underlying "what people will say" plant in us an image of what a good person is and does.[18]

William Willimon says that in addition to guiding behavior, gossip can be a primary means of building and sustaining communities. As the new member is included in the gossip, bonds are created that indicate that she or he now belongs.

Community cannot emerge without intimacy, and gossip enables people to explore the lives of others. Shared intimacy leads to bonding, not only by linking those who share through gossip but also by linking us to the life of the one who is being gossiped about. . . . [Gossip] enlarges our grasp of someone else's experience and thereby increases our understanding of ourselves. A congregation that doesn't know intimate information about one another isn't much of a church.[19]

However, when it is deceptive, arbitrary, and mean-spirited, gossip can be damaging rather than community building. Personal information shared in a prayer circle can promote healing as "godsibb"—or spill out as cruel gossip.

Like rumors, gossip can reflect leadership's preoccupation with controlling the information available, internally within the congregation and externally to the public. When Jennifer filed a complaint against her pastor, Ed, for sexual misconduct, the denomination immediately began its formal investigation process, and Jennifer was told to keep silent to ensure a fair investigation. However, as the denominational officials attempted to control all related information from start to finish, they never told the congregation why the pastor had suddenly taken a leave. Lacking the whole story, members of the congregation began to piece together an explanation.

Gossip erupted about Ed's departure and the attractive divorcee, Jennifer, who stopped attending church at the same time. Word spread of a possible romance and her recent depression. Facts were woven into gossip. People speculated that Jennifer was desperate to "get a man," so "obviously" she was out to destroy Pastor Ed after he had spurned her flirtations. Overcontrol of information, no matter how well intentioned, often creates more confusion and fertile ground for fabricated or misinterpreted facts.

A few weeks later someone in the congregation searched the Web for Ed's name and discovered that in a congregation Ed had formerly served he had been sued by a man whose wife Ed had enticed into an affair. The communication drama would have been greatly reduced had denominational officials shared that easily accessible and verifiable information with the congregation in the beginning, given church members information about the professional ethics expected of clergy, and explained the denominational process for handling complaints. Curiosity about who might be the target of the pastor's boundary violation is difficult to stop, but the gossip would have been reduced and would have been kinder, and the rumors would have been minimized. Once trust in denominational officials has been eroded by their withholding information and by the whirling gossip and rumors that filled the void, anything communicated by the denomination from that point on lacks credibility—not because it is untrue, but because the people have developed their own "facts."

Problems with Rumors and Gossip

Both rumors and gossip

- spread potentially inaccurate or misinterpreted information that may be difficult to verify
- are difficult to control because of their informal nature and disregard for appropriate lines of communication

- disseminate easily through e-mails, blogs, parking-lot conversations, and phone calls
- damage sources of accurate information
- are magnified by including anonymous others and fabricated details
- create divisiveness, increased anxiety, and reactivity
- deflect or distract attention, time, and energy from real problems in the congregation
- entertain the gossiper, rumormonger, and/or the consumer, but certainly not those who are the subject
- are used to gain self-esteem, allies, or perceived power
- are exploitative when used by one person to gain an advantage over another
- indicate the leadership's possible secret keeping or preoccupation with controlling available information, internally to the congregation and externally to the public

---

Exposure

Sometimes a group is exposed to too much information rather than too little, and when too much information is available, someone is bound to feel exposed. On the family vacation to Disney World, a friend got stopped for speeding on the long, straight interstate through the middle of Florida. As he tried to negotiate his way out of a ticket, his four-year-old daughter chirped up in the backseat, "I told Daddy over and over to slow down. He was going really, really fast. I told him he was being bad." Overdisclosure of some information can be just as problematic in congregations as it was for this dad!

Usually too much information is inconsequential, unless it includes personal data that would normally be reserved for a more intimate or confidential relationship. Then the hearer feels exposed to information in a public setting that the culture deems to be private. For example, during an hour session of pastoral counseling with a couple, a pastor told a detailed story about a recent fight with his wife. This inappropriate counseling technique diverted attention from the issue that the couple came to deal with and provided them with too much personal information about the pastor. The couple left the session questioning the pastor's credibility to handle a problem such as theirs.

Every relationship has an inherent standard about the limit of personal information that is appropriate to share. That limit in business or professional relationships differs from the limit in relationships with an intimate partner or trusted, lifelong friend. Under the guise of sexual education, a youth minister explicitly described to the high school group his sexual relationship with his girlfriend. This gave them way too much information.

Sometimes the person who is the topic of the exposure does not choose to be exposed. If a judicatory official wants to know if a pastor is going to therapy, the question might be appropriate in private conversation but not in front of the pastor's personnel committee. No matter what the pastor's response, the pastor could look bad to those who think he needs therapy but is afraid to go or to those who, in discovering that he is in therapy, wonder what his problems are. In addition to the pastor's feeling exposed, that degree of personal information may be more than the personnel committee needs to know.

Unlike rumors, exposures involve accurate information—just too much information. Some exposure may result from innocent encouragement in a prayer group to be open and forthright as Christians. Some exposure may be shared out of loneliness in a genuine desire to be fully known. For example, a new member hoping to assimilate into a fresh congregation may prematurely choose confidants. Some overexposure may result from simply not understanding appropriate limits for personal information.

After Rachel had survived years of sexual abuse by her father, child protective services placed her with a foster family near Brown Mountain Church. Because of all the secrets in her family of origin, she had no experience with informational boundaries, so she easily slipped from one extreme to another—from withholding all personal stories to telling too many. After, and sometimes during, every gathering of the high school group, the youth pastor coached her about what was appropriate public conversation. The pastor knew that overdisclosure of personal information leaves both the hearer and the speaker feeling uncomfortable, exposed, and vulnerable. For Rachel, the information she blurted out could later be used against her to feed gossip or ridicule.

How much information is too much? Current Internet technologies such as e-mail, chat rooms, and blogs encourage exposure. Because the writer cannot see the recipient's reaction, these communications are sometimes more intimate than direct person-to-person conversation. The sender lacks the visual cues that indicate that too much as been shared. In addition, today's reality and tell-all television shows distort our perceptions about what is appropriate to know about and say about individuals.

Exposure is often well-intentioned. For example, in December, leaders of one church's building campaign decided to leave donors' pledge and financial statements in the narthex of the church for members to pick up. That way they would save postage and avoid possible loss of statements in the piles of Christmas mail. Jim, a member of the congregation who was on an extended business assignment in another state, wanted to send a check to the building campaign before the end of the tax year, but he couldn't remember how much he had already given towards his pledge. Jim had his mail forwarded, but of course didn't get his pledge statement because those were sitting in the church narthex. So he called the church office and asked for an accounting.

The pastor said that the financial person who had the information was on vacation, so he would send an e-mail to members of the committee to see if anyone knew Jim's pledge amount and payments. Anxious that so many would know about his inability to keep track of his own finances, Jim was angry about the church's trying to save a stamp or two on financial statements and the pastor's lack of knowledge and sensitivity about financial issues. But most of all, Jim felt exposed by a whole committee exchanging e-mails about his giving. Having so many people discussing his private finances, especially using the Internet, lowered his trust in the congregational leadership's discretion.

Leaks

Some information protected by faith tradition, policy, or congregational practice may leak out anyway. Usually this unauthorized dissemination of information relates to a breach in confidentiality or crossing other agreed-upon boundaries. Leaks not only convey too much information but also violate trust between those who had previously agreed to hold the information. The unfortunate reality is that stories leak out of personnel committee meetings, leadership meetings about difficult decisions, pastor search committees, and prayer groups, even though promises have been made to protect the information forever or for a specified time period.

Leaks may be intentional or unintentional, calculated or accidental. In a ministerial support group, a pastor learned that a colleague was having an affair with a staff member. Though anything said in the room was supposed to stay in the room, the pastor was so ashamed of his colleague's behavior, he mentioned him and the staff member during the Sunday pastoral prayer, using their names. His prayer precipitated the exposure of the secret affair and ultimately the firing of both the staff person and the pastor.

Such intentional leaks are often an unconscious attempt to gain power by someone who feels powerless. The pastor may have felt powerless to stop his colleague's destructive actions, he so used information that was out-of-bounds. People gain social status by being in the know about key information and knowing who else knows the information. An anonymous donor occasionally made large gifts to Temple Beth Shalom, but a couple of people figured out who he was and realized the value of that information. His name was carefully leaked only to those in an inner circle of leaders who could then use that knowledge to sway decisions about congregational building renovations and future direction. Just as money is power, so was the information about who had that money and how to access it.

Often leaks happen naively and without forethought about consequences to individuals and the congregation. Even inadvertently broken agreements about protecting information severely damage trust and therefore relationships. Leaders are held to a higher standard because of the responsibility of their position, so when they leak information, their ability to effectively lead the congregation is crippled by the resulting lack of confidence. Leaks are breaches of fiduciary responsibility.

Committees and prayer groups need to review disclosure agreements and limitations regularly to ensure privacy. Usually all involved agree not to discuss what happens in these closed sessions, even with a spouse or partner. But leaks are tempting, and particularly common in the marriage dyad, when one partner sits on a congregational committee that needs to hold closed meetings because of the sensitivity of the information discussed.

Leaks can create conflict, distrust, confusion, and worst of all, betrayal. Without trust, congregations cannot become *communities* of faith. So agreement about what and how information is shared, not only verbally but also in writing, is crucial for congregations. The clearer the boundaries for releasing information, the less likely those boundaries will be ignored by someone leaking protected information. The clearer the understanding as to why that information is protected, the less likely those boundaries will be violated. When Marcia explained to her husband why she couldn't share any names or details about the fascinating candidates for the rector's position and the difficulty she was having *not* telling him, he appreciated what she was allowed to tell him about the recruitment process, and he grew to accept that he had to wait for a full report.

Congregational leaders need to manage information with intentionality. To whom does the information belong? Who will be helped by the sharing and who could be harmed? How much will be revealed? When? What needs to be protected and for how long? Chapters 8 and 9 help faith leaders make information-management decisions and craft agreements for information dissemination.

Out-of-Bounds Communication

Congregations often replicate enmeshed families where, rather than talk directly to someone, people communicate indirectly through gossip, rumor, exposure, or leaks. These out-of-bounds techniques for passing on information help the gossiper, rumormonger, exposer, or leaker to gain power and dodge responsibility for the potential damage the information has on others. When people are afraid to face the consequences their behavior has on others and are afraid to be challenged in return, they turn to these indirect patterns. Someone engaged in this behavior often explains, "I just don't want to hurt anyone's feelings" or "I just hate confrontation." Instead of allowing these cop-outs for out-of-bounds communication, congregations must stop bad communication habits and inappropriate concealing and revealing of information by isolating or challenging individuals who regularly use harmful strategies. For healthy information management, congregational leaders must teach everyone courageous first-person, truth-filled communication.

Chapter 5

Levels of Information

Remember learning taxonomy in high school biology? Or maybe by grade school you already knew the difference between a reptile and a mammal. Without classifying animals into broader categories, from species to genus to family, understanding more complicated facts about them would be impossible. By organizing congregation-related information in a similar way, congregational leaders benefit from distinctions between various levels of information. The taxonomy of information depends simply on the number of individuals who know the information. The number of people in the know may include only one person protecting her innermost dreams, as many as an entire congregation, or everyone in town who reads the local newspaper.

To minimize the potential damage caused by disseminating sensitive information and to maximize the overall well-being of the congregation, the decision to increase the number of people who know requires careful thought and judgment. As information is passed on to more people, the process cannot be reversed. Valerie, a daughter of a charismatic priest, felt called into ministry herself but she never told anyone else about her dreams because she convinced herself that she could never be as effective as her father. Finally, Valerie mentioned going to seminary to a friend, sure that her friend would reinforce her sense of unworthiness. Instead, the friend rejoiced, and then two people knew. But going to seminary

meant telling her pastor, so the circle of those knowing about her
call to ministry widened to three. Eventually one committee after
another heard her story, from the school's admission committee to
the ordination discernment committee at her church. Finally, Valerie went public and was eventually ordained. Like Valerie's sense
of call, all information regardless of its content can be categorized
by how many people know it at any given time.

Categorizing information into levels does not necessarily make
decisions about its management easier. The more sensitive the in-
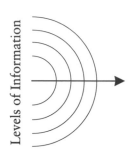 formation, the more discernment is required
congregational leaders each time the number
people who know expands. What if Valerie's
hope to be ordained were more volatile information? Let's say her faith tradition did
ordain women or she were lesbian and the
nomination did not ordain homosexuals.
Then the news of her call might have cre-
ated tension or outright conflict within her congregation and have
required more careful and prudent consideration.

Levels of Information Disclosure

Private   Information known by only one person who
                   therefore owns it.

Confidential   Information released to a second person, usu-
                   ally with assurances that it will not be shared
                   with anyone beyond the two without expressed
                   or written permission.

Limited access   Information known by three or more people
                   but protected from distribution by agreements
                   protecting it.

| Open | Information shared openly with the congregation yet not easily accessible to the public. |
| Public | Information easily accessible and widespread, such as news reports and criminal records. |

Private Material

Private information is information owned by one person who alone can determine whether to share it. It is what we know about ourselves and choose not to share with others. Each of us has an internal world of memories, hopes, faith, thoughts, prayers, history, opinions, and fears. In the realm of human sexuality, sexual fantasy and preferences are extremely private. Behavior not witnessed by others is private. Our privacy may be related to something we would prefer others not know because we are ashamed of it, whether it be self-doubt or an addiction to Internet shopping, or we may simply choose to keep it to ourselves. All this private material is unique to us and makes us individual.

Because our private material defines who we are as individuals, it also gives us the power to influence how others see us and to determine the direction of our lives. We choose what private information to release and what to protect. Marilyn wanted people to see her as ethical and intelligent, so never told anyone that she had cheated on the Episcopal general ordination exam that was required before priesthood. In the first church she served, she realized that the community was much more liberal politically, so she kept her conservative opinions to herself. By controlling what personal information others knew about her, she could create the persona she desired.

Sometimes the way we protect our private inner space may be dangerous to our health and safety and the health and safety of others when it becomes a harmful escape or a way to avoid facing problems constructively. Or worse, we may conceal suicidal plans or addictions. Privacy takes on the toxicity of secrecy when the concept of having a private emotional or physical space shifts from helping us individuate to hiding aspects of our selves or our lives out of shame. Healthy privacy transforms into dangerous secrecy when a teen tucks drugs under his mattress or an older member of the congregation who lives alone refuses to allow a visiting deacon into her home for fear the deacon will discover that she can no longer take care of herself.

Private Information

- is known by only one person, its owner
- may be shared by that person or kept private
- should not be revealed or concealed by force, but at the free will of its owner

---

Confidential Information

When we share private information about ourselves with another person, verbally or in writing, the communication moves to the level of confidentiality. Two people know.

Between close friends, one friend might ask the other to promise never to tell anyone else what was just shared. While we describe sexual intimacy as private, if two people are involved in it, the exchange is technically confidential. Friends and intimate partners have informal confidentiality agreements.

Confidentiality agreements in faith communities are more formal. Because congregants trust clergy with intimate information, clergy become "information trustees." Most faith traditions have policies and states have civil laws that delineate the fiduciary responsibility that clergy have as trustees of the personal information they are told. These codes of confidentiality encourage trust in the clergy, protect strictly personal information from third parties, and allow for confessional communication between a religious confessor and individuals eager to purge their souls by truth telling. Clergy confidentiality is intended to help individuals overcome personal problems so as not to cause further harm to themselves or others. Therefore, many faith traditions require clergy to disclose someone's personal information if that person is at risk of harming himself or herself or someone else. Learning the specific rules of their own religious body along with legal requirements for reporting suspected abuse in their state is essential for faith leaders. (Chapter 7 includes an in-depth look at confidentiality and the law.)

Rarely do congregations understand the ramifications of the confidentiality policies of their faith traditions. Most congregants assume that anything said to a clergyperson will not be repeated. To avoid confusion or feelings of betrayal, clergy should make sure that congregational members understand the limit of what is confidential and what is not. Therapists usually hand a new client a printed description of the agreements necessary for an effective therapist-client relationship. Among other details, that paper outlines the boundaries of confidentiality within their conversations. Clergy can do likewise and explain in writing the circumstances in which they would share confidential information with legal, ecclesiastical, or supervisory authorities.

Because denominational guidelines and legal mandates can be confusing, a good way to establish general principles for the congregation is for the clergy and representative lay leaders to develop guidelines about confidentiality and publish them in a flyer, bulletin, or newsletter article. Local congregational guidelines about confidentiality should address how personal information will be protected, based on

- its content (Is anyone at risk of harm?)

- its owner (Did the person give permission for the information to be shared?)
- the context in which the information is shared and with whom, and whether the intent of the sharing is confessional (as defined by that faith tradition)
- any applicable canon or denominational rules and civil laws

If those guidelines do not address breaking confidentiality when harm has been done or is likely to be done, then the local congregation's policy can be even more specific. Such a congregational policy at the local level may state:

> This congregation values the worth of every individual, and we understand that it is our ethical duty to protect each member or visitor from harm. If you tell one of our ordained or lay ministers that a child or dependent adult has been harmed or is at risk of harm or that you may hurt yourself or someone else, we will share that information with legal authorities who can intervene. This information will be disclosed according to state mandates for reporting child, elder, and disabled or dependent adult abuse and according to the ethical standards of practice for ministry professionals. Confidentiality will be maintained about any and all information not directly related to the concern for safety.

Congregations may fear that a policy like this will reduce the sharing that leads to closer relationships and community building, but those who have such policies find that they enhance trust rather than limit the personal information given to pastoral leaders. In addition, such a policy and practice highlight the congregation's commitment to creating sanctuary for every individual. With a statement like the one above, people from the community may drop by the pastor's office for counseling or pastoral care and know that the information shared will have confidentiality limits.

Like privacy, confidentiality can also become dangerous—when it is used as a cloak to cover secrets or as a strategy to dodge accountability. Protecting individuals from the consequences of their actions denies them the opportunity for spiritual repentance and change. Members of the congregation are similarly denied the opportunity to make changes if crucial information is withheld from them in the erroneous name of confidentiality. To the detriment of congregational health, faith leaders tend to err on the side of hiding vital information, even when individuals' safety may be involved.

When only two individuals, such as the church's pastor and treasurer, know that the church's light bill isn't being paid, that information is not appropriately kept confidential, although each might be tempted to do so. The pastor, fearful that the church will oust him for declining worship attendance, may not share financial problems with other leaders. The treasurer may feel vulnerable to allegations that she was skimming off the top and choose to protect the information. Keeping the information between the pastor and treasurer is a way to avoid criticism or responsibility; however, it is not confidentiality. Transparency within a congregation regarding *any* information affecting its governance, health, and integrity is the goal for which to strive.

For clergy, confidentiality issues involve more than their conversations with congregational members. One-on-one supervision of an employee, student intern, or candidate for ministry might include conversations between only the two people present. The information revealed in those sessions might be confidential forever or may eventually need to be shared with another person or committee. When expectations of confidentiality are not made explicit, situations may arise in which one party does not realize what is expected and releases information that results in harm or potential harm. Therefore, how confidential information will be managed is as important to spell out clearly in these situations as in conversations between a clergyperson and congregant.

Confidential Information

- is information released to a second person
- is protected by assurances that it will not be shared with a third person without the confidant's permission or in accordance with state law, denominational guidelines, and congregational policies
- is not the same as secret keeping or withholding information another person needs or has a right to receive

---

Limited-Access Information

Some seemingly confidential information needs to be shared with individuals other than the two in the original conversation or situation. When discussed with or witnessed by a third party, the information is no longer confidential or held by only an informant and the listener. Information known by two or more people, however sensitive or personal, becomes "limited-access" information. For example, a congregant may tell both the minister and the church treasurer about personal financial difficulties. This limited-access information is known by more than two people but is still protected from more general dissemination.

To prevent conflict or distrust, each potential increase in the number of people who know certain information requires intentional discernment about whether to expand the circle. The greater the number of people who know the information, the greater the potential for inappropriate spreading of the information. Therefore the decision to share the information with a new person or group needs to be considered wisely.

Limited-access information may be known by as few as three people but expands as the number of people who know increases.

If a copier repairperson sexually harasses a secretary working at a synagogue, the harassment may at first be known only by the repairperson and the secretary—but then becomes limited-access information when the secretary tells the rabbi. As her supervisor, the rabbi is required by law and by congregational policy to respond and to stop the harassment. Therefore he must disclose the story to the appropriate leaders. When the rabbi tells the personnel chairperson, the president of the congregation, and the congregation administrator, the information is still considered limited access. Even though the number of those who know about the sexual harassment has increased, the number is still restricted. When the personnel committee discusses an appropriate response and the congregation administrator calls the repairperson's supervisor, the number of those who know increases further. As each new person is informed, more people have the sensitive information.

Discernment is crucial in determining not only *who* else needs to know the information but also *what* needs to be told. As a decision is made to increase the number of people who know certain information, a decision must also be made about the amount of detail to reveal. As information is appropriately passed on to more people, the amount of information shared is usually less than what was revealed in the previous layer of limited-access information or might be shared in a confidential communication. When information is sensitive, only what is essential should be shared. When the rabbi tells the appropriate congregational leaders about the sexual harassment, he shares the smallest amount of information necessary for adequate response, unless the secretary gives him permission for more disclosure. So appropriately shared limited-access information is limited in the number of those knowing it, but as that number increases the details and content of what is known decreases.

Prayer or cluster groups in congregations may pledge confidentiality, but really the agreement means what is discussed in the group is limited-access information. Usually nothing said in the context of the group may be mentioned beyond those individuals in attendance (limiting the number of those *who* know) or anything repeated must avoid any specifics that might reveal the identity of another person (limiting *what* others know). Some groups abide by an agreement not to repeat a story from the group without the permission of the person who owns the story. When extremely delicate materials are discussed, the group may agree to not discuss anything brought up in the group when outside the group's meeting space—not even if the members of the group are standing in the parking lot or relaxing over coffee. But certainly in small groups, more than two people know the information discussed, so it is hardly confidential.

Another form of limited-access information containment is the practice of anonymity. Anonymity is helpful when a congregational leader seeks the wisdom of a professional consultant, therapist, or colleague to resolve a congregational or pastoral problem. Three people have access to this information—the congregational leader, the consultant, and the individual(s) about whom the consultation is called. The leader shares only the amount of information needed to receive the best advice. Names and details may be left out or changed to protect the identity of any individuals whose personal material is being discussed. Neither the person asking for profes- sional advice nor the one giving it should share more information than necessary for the consultation. Sharing unnecessary aspects of a story can create problems.

One accountant gave too much information to his clergy client when he explained that some tax deductions for clergy are marginal, if not unethical. The example he gave was about another client who successfully deducted a church-related party on his income tax form the previous year. He said that the client had been a bishop and named the diocese, which was sufficient data to reveal his identity. The pastor realized that the accountant was talking about her uncle!

Limits on certain information include how many people know, how much they know, and a specified time during which the in- formation is not shared with others. A candidate for a pastoral position may share information with one member of the search committee and request that others not be informed immediately. Such information is confidential between those two individuals for a time and then becomes limited access if revealed to the whole search committee and later, if appropriate, to the governing body. If parts of the information are determined to be important to share with the congregation, then the information may later become open.

When Cynthia interviewed for a ministerial position in Kansas, she privately mentioned to one search committee member that she had recently completed chemotherapy and would have to fly back to Georgia for ongoing monthly checkups. She asked that the information not be shared just yet, because she didn't want to get the position out of sympathy, nor did she want to be disqualified immediately due to worries about her health. After she was among the final choices for the position, Cynthia, to avoid secret keeping, told the whole committee. The committee decided that her ongoing recovery would not affect her job performance and that she, not they, could choose who else should know and when.

Limited-Access Information

- is known by more than two people, but still protected from general knowledge
- may originally have been confidential information
- may expand in the number of people with access to it
- usually involves more limited detail than confidential information as more people receive the information
- is usually protected for a specified amount of time (from a brief period of time to permanently)

Reasons to expand the number of people who have certain information vary. The most common reasons are (1) to protect vulnerable individuals from harm, (2) to receive professional consultation, or (3) to deal with personnel or other difficult congregational issues. As mentioned earlier, many faith traditions allow, recommend, or require disclosure of confidential information to avert harm or abuse to individuals or the community. Several states include clergy and other faith leaders among those professions required to report suspected abuse. These legal and ethical codes state when and what government agencies need to be notified, as well as how the information will be protected from further disclosure.

Sometimes faith leaders find themselves faced with problems far beyond their range of experience or expertise. Handling the challenge as a lone ranger may have dire consequences, so the situation may require the advice of a professional consultant, a therapist, or a supervisor. Even if getting that advice means moving previously confidential information to the level of limited access, personal details still can be protected.

When Rev. Halloway struggled with a difficult pastoral situation in his congregation, he called both his insurance company and a professional consultant to discuss the problem. Though he protected the specific names involved and only shared enough detail to gain the guidance he needed, he moved confidential information to the level of limited access. Insurance representatives and consultants (if they are well trained and ethical) will not share such information with others.

Dealing with personnel or other difficult congregational issues often requires that information become limited access. Responsible committee work requires that group members understand appropriate limits to information access. Often committees say they will maintain confidentiality, but they really mean, "Let's limit who knows this." The team planning a surprise party for the anniversary of the priest's ordination limits who knows about the plans until the invitations are sent. Then information is still limited to the invitation list and the priest still isn't told. Never has the information been confidential—simply limited.

Using the term *confidentiality* when something else is meant creates confusion. Trust erodes in congregations if confidentiality really means keeping secrets or watching out that so-and-so doesn't find out something. Misinformed use of the term *confidentiality* inhibits individuals from turning to their clergy for truly confidential conversations. To be more accurate, committees working on sensitive issues might say, "This information is limited right now, because . . ." For example, instead of erroneously claiming confidentiality, the chairperson of the search committee for the new rabbi may tell a curious member of the congregation, "We are not able to discuss details right now, but I can say we're reading through applications." "Well, did Rabbi Miller apply?" the eager member asks. "We are not able to discuss details right now," the chairperson repeats, "but you are welcome to check with Rabbi Miller directly."

Most committees would benefit from training and experience in setting boundaries around the information they must process. Continuously revisiting the question, "Who should know what when?" would help committees determine appropriate limits regarding (1) which individuals or groups should be informed, (2) how much detail is necessary when they are informed, and (3) how long the limits set around the information will stay in place.

The stewardship committee learned that Jackson, one of their members, refused to participate in individual solicitation, but Jackson was embarrassed about his strong aversion, so he asked the group not to mention it to anyone else. He had earlier explained to his pastor that he and his wife had gotten into a painful argument one year when someone from the church dropped by to ask for his pledge. That was confidential sharing between Jackson and the pastor. He gave a briefer rendition of the story to the stewardship committee and defined the limits of the access of this information: "Please don't say *anything* to *anyone* about this *ever*." The committee honored his request to limit what was known, who knew, and for how long.

Personnel issues involve various types of information that can be troublesome. The congregation's office manager, Leanne, realized that her administrative assistant was messing up on the job but had covered for him enough times that no one else really knew about it. The fact of his incompetence was virtually confidential information. She finally mentioned the problems to the personnel committee chairperson, who informed the committee at its next meeting. The information about the inept employee stayed within the limits of the committee for several months while efforts were made to improve his performance. When goals for improvement failed, the committee expanded the limits of those who knew about the problem to the whole governing body of the congregation, who agreed with the committee's recommendation to ask for his resignation. Though some members wanted to know more specifics out of curiosity, only enough details were shared to explain the problem and the recommended solution. Leanne also explained there had been no abuse and no mismanagement of funds or other egregious behavior. When the administrative assistant resigned, the governing body could truthfully explain that there had been a mismatch between the employee's skills and those needed for such a position.

Legally and ethically appropriate situations for moving information from confidential to limited access may include the following:

- Averting serious harm and/or protecting an innocent third party
- Safeguarding the community or subsequent employer against danger
- Meeting legal or ethical requirements, including mandated reporting of abuse or suicidal or homicidal intentions
- Receiving legal or professional consultations
- Sharing pastoral care issues with others, with the individual's permission
- Doing relevant, responsible committee work
- Effectively managing some personnel issues

Open Information

Some information needs to be shared with a broader audience—the staff, leaders, and members of the congregation; other congregations; or the general public. "Open" information is known by a broad group of people but not the general public. No agreements, rules, or guidelines protect further dissemination of this information, yet it is not as easily discovered as public information (discussed below). The church secretary may be told about the Tuesday Bible study with the expectation that he will put an announcement in the Sunday bulletin. The information is open for others to freely know, but unless information about the class appears on the church Web site, the likelihood that anyone outside the church knows about it is doubtful. So the information is open but not publicly known. Many congregations assume that announcements to their members about pending events make them public knowledge, but as much as congregants might talk, the knowledge usually stays in house.

As an example of moving from confidential to open information, consider a senior rector who goes to the personnel committee for consultation over repeated difficulties with the associate rector. The personnel committee members must hold that limited-access information, not sharing it with spouses, friends, or other church leaders. If the personnel committee finds the problems irresolvable, the information (not the unnecessary details) may need to be shared with the congregation's governing body (the vestry) to determine whether the associate's ministry in that setting may continue. As the personnel committee did earlier, the vestry now needs to hold the limited-access information among its own members, not sharing it with spouses, friends, or other church leaders.

If the vestry ultimately determines that the associate needs to be dismissed, the whole congregation needs to know the recommendation of its elected leaders, but usually not the details or full discussion. When the vestry takes its recommendation to remove the associate pastor to the congregation, the information expands from limited access to open, even though the congregation is a defined entity and may want to protect the information. Limiting dissemination at this point is impossible.

When information is discussed in a forum such as a congregational meeting, in essence it loses all protections against its being repeated. Any limits on information sharing are now voluntary, not restricted by written or spoken agreements about who can be told or what can be shared. Church leaders might ask that only official members attend the congregational meeting and that those present honor the sensitivity of the material they might be hearing. Yet, with no sanctions against the information being repeated, the vestry cannot be assured that it stays in house. Conversations between spouses and partners, with neighbors and friends, and among church members are expected. Thus, letters to a congregation; congregational meetings; and discussions at worship, in the fellowship hall, or in open meetings are in the realm of open information. Opening information requires discernment about how and when the information is opened, to whom the information is opened (other congregations or the general public), and what is shared.

Congregations benefit from as much open information as possible. Transparency builds trust, helps the leaders govern more effectively, and encourages clearer communication. As open information increases, rumors and gossip decrease—and appropriate confidentiality is maintained instead of secrets being kept. If information is overly protected, rumors or gossip may bridge the gaps, but because rumors lack accuracy and gossip can be mean-spirited, they often fuel confusion and conflict. As in all information sharing, prudence guides the appropriate amount of detail to be shared, timing of disclosures, and who has a need and a right to know what information. Open information does not mean that everyone knows it, needs to know it, or even wants to know it—only that it is available to be known and is not protected from being spread.

When a congregation discovered that a volunteer adult youth leader had been sending inappropriate e-mail notes to one of its teens, the pastor and personnel committee immediately responded. The youth leader was asked to leave the position and to have no further contact with any of the youth in the congregation. Upon learning that the youth and her parents had taken legal action, the pastor also consulted a lawyer. The accused adult was a well-loved and respected leader in the congregation and community, and the pastor knew that what could be said about the incident had to be carefully considered. What appeared in the local paper was public, of course. But access to some information, such as specific documentation about the incident, had to be limited, and the pastor's individual communications with the alleged perpetrator and with the victim were confidential.

As the pastor struggled over what to do, he decided to make as much information as transparent as possible. He consulted the lawyer, asked the alleged victim what she felt comfortable sharing, and then put his own correspondence and minutes of meetings related to the situation in a notebook that stayed on his desk. Then when members of the congregation asked about the situation, he described the allegations in a few sentences and explained the steps taken to handle the situation. Church members could visit the pastor's office during regular office hours and review the minutes and letters of correspondence if they wanted to do so. This kept the congregation safer from accusations of slander or libel by the accused, while making as much information as possible available to concerned individuals.

Transparency is especially crucial during congregational crises, when opening as much information as possible helps prevent escalation of the tension and prevents the rewounding that occurs if more secrets are later discovered. Information opened in a clear and timely manner also creates opportunities for reconciliation and renewal in the congregation. However, when information is leaked out rather than intentionally and carefully disseminated by congregational leaders, crises intensify as the misinformation, distrust, and conflict increase.

Open Information

- is known by more than two people and unprotected from further sharing with others
- is usually more limited than confidential or limited-access information in the amount of detail shared
- is not easily accessible by the general public
- includes leaks of information and other uncontrolled dissemination
- could lead to allegations of slander or libel if the intention for opening the information can be proven to be malicious

---

Public Information

Public information is easily accessible to anyone. It is what you read in newspapers or hear in other media reports. You can browse for it on the Internet. At the county courthouse, the public can obtain many legal records, such as criminal arrests and charges; court decisions; civil proceedings; and records of birth, death, marriage, and divorce. Each state has enacted government codes that grant the public a broad right of access to public records while protecting legitimate governmental interests and the privacy rights of individual citizens. Anyone can know public information; anyone can spread it.

The public has the right to know the information but not necessarily the right to spread it around recklessly. For example, if someone learned that a registered sex offender was attending a congregation and put up flyers with the offender's picture on bulletin boards all around the facility, this overreaction could be grounds for a lawsuit. (Chapter 11 explores better strategies for handling information about sex offenders in congregations.)

Although public information may be readily available, congregational leaders may choose not to know it. Although Megan's Law has made sex offender registries public in every state, some congregations still refuse to use the registry to screen potential volunteers to work with children, youth, and vulnerable adults. That choice increases the likelihood of child abuse and negligence lawsuits. Some congregations choose not to scan the register for members or visitors who might be listed. One mistaken pastor complained that using the registry violates the person's privacy, even though the registry is public record. Another minister said he simply didn't want to know about any convicted sex offenders in his congregation because he was overwhelmed and uncertain what to do with that information. Either excuse ignores information that is publicly accessible and leaves the congregation open to potential crisis.

Public Information

- is easily accessible to large numbers of people without restriction (may come from the Internet or newspaper)
- includes what state and federal statutes declare open to the community (such as criminal and civil records)
- may be easily accessed but legal and ethical considerations restrains its dissemination

---

Understanding these five levels of information—private, confidential, limited access, open, and public—and the dynamics at each level prepares congregational leaders to make wise information management decisions. The perception of secrecy damages the overall health of congregations, while transparency and appropriate disclosures build healthy congregations and create a sense of sanctuary. When faithful people tell their intimate stories in community, talk about their relationship with God, and share soulfully, their communications must be honored. Those intimate stories must be handled with wisdom, maximizing privacy while minimizing secrecy and preventing harm. When leaders clarify their communication processes and hold themselves accountable for the information they receive and share, trust and integrity within the congregation grow. Transparency, balanced with respect for personal privacy, enhances congregational health.

Chapter 6

Access to Information

An investment company marketed its services with the line, "Curious minds want to know." The line was effective because it is true. Curiosity drives the technology revolution, which continues to expand the boundaries of knowledge. What information is necessary for congregations? To help curious faith leaders increase the amount of information available to them and their congregations for their mutual ministries, this chapter describes the legal principle of "right to know" and the ethical principle of "need to know."

Right to Know

The "right to know" is a relatively recent legal concept, explained more often by example than by formal definition. A right is an entitlement, freedom, power, or privilege to do or to know something. Yet even in a democracy, people have rights to certain information but not all information. Permission to access information about a congregation's financial records, minutes of meetings, and names and addresses of members may be granted by the congregation or its judicatory, while other information may be protected. "Right to know" pertains to information individuals are justly entitled to by civil code or denominational guidelines.

The Right to Know Congregation-Related Information

Who has a right to know certain information about a congregation and its work can be illustrated using layered triangles.

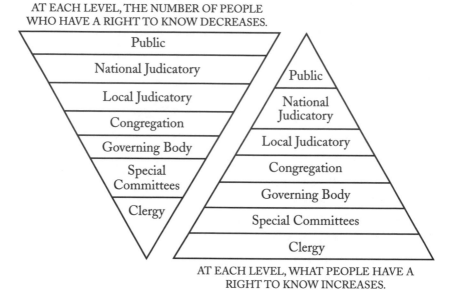

AT EACH LEVEL, THE NUMBER OF PEOPLE
WHO HAVE A RIGHT TO KNOW DECREASES.

AT EACH LEVEL, WHAT PEOPLE HAVE A
RIGHT TO KNOW INCREASES.

FIGURE 6.1
WHO HAS A RIGHT TO KNOW?
HOW MUCH DO THEY HAVE A RIGHT TO KNOW?

As illustrated, at each level, from the public to a special committee of a congregation, the number of individuals knowing the information *decreases* as the amount of information *increases*. The public knows the least amount of information about a congregation; a small stewardship committee or clergy may know the most.

State and federal laws require congregations to report employee compensation. Beyond that limited, legally required information, faith groups themselves determine who has access to information about their congregations and what those people can know. They may share a great deal of information, going as far as publicly offering information on denominational or congregational Web sites or in print. So the general public may include the largest number of people with general information, but the public has a right to know the least amount of specific information about a religious entity.

As the number of people with a right to know decreases, the information available about a congregation increases. A congregation's national or international governing body usually has right to know more about a congregation than the public, but less than the local judicatory (the diocese, conference, synod, and the like). The local judicatory of a congregation usually has a right to know everything the public does about a congregation, as well as everything the higher governing body knows, but not as much as the congregation members themselves can know, depending on the polity of their faith tradition.

A right-to-know question may arise about who can obtain copies of minutes from the governing body of a congregation. The general public does not have the right to see the official records of governing body of a congregation (the session, council, vestry, and the like), because the public is neither governed nor directly affected by that body. Minutes are considered public records only when a legal case involving the congregation is before the court. Along with leaders, members may see the meeting minutes of their congregation's governing body. Yet in some denominations the judicatory has no right to read a congregation's minutes.

Alice saw herself as the matriarch of Westwood United Church of Christ and privy to all critical information about the congregation. She expected to know everything from the pastor's schedule to the specific reason certain parishioners were in the hospital. When the church council declared a closed session to discuss a difficult issue, other church members were denied access to information about that discussion. The church president nearly lost his patience trying to explain to Alice that, because she was not an elected leader, she had no right to know certain official business of the church. She refused to believe that some sensitive information, such as personnel issues or donor records, was restricted to very few designated individuals—that is, members of the congregation's personnel and stewardship committees. Alice caused such a turmoil that the church decided to add a section to their communication policy that clarified who had a right to know what. Although she never calmed down about being left out of the loop, others in the congregation appreciated discussion and transparency about church governance and information boundaries.

Both civil and denominational rules apply to personally sensitive information, such as personnel records. Personnel records should be kept in locked files and strictly controlled, though individuals usually have access to their own files and the right to add things to them. The material should not be retained beyond carefully set time limits. Advice about access to files and their maintenance can be obtained by consulting with human-resources specialists or through legal counsel. When searching for new staff, personnel committees should also consider who has a right to know the information collected about each candidate and how it will be disposed of after the search is complete.

Franklin was thrilled when his wife began serving on the search committee for the new senior rector—but then grew frustrated when she told him that every committee meeting ended with a reminder that no information about any of the candidates being reviewed should leave the meeting, even after the name of the final candidate was ready for recommendation. Franklin tried to tease his wife into leaking some hints, but he wasn't successful. He later learned the seriousness of protecting personnel and personal information when he became responsible for handling the church's screening process for potential volunteers to work with children. Then he had to carefully guard the results of interviews, conversations with references, and criminal background checks. He knew from his business experience that faith leaders on search, personnel, and screening committees should check with human-resources specialists or employment lawyers to determine who has a right to know personal information about staff and volunteers and how information is protected from dissemination.

The chart in the appendix shows individuals and groups of people who have a right to certain information about a congregation at that level.

The Right to Know Information about an Individual

The right to know personal information is much more protected than information about a congregation or religious institution. Someone's arrest record, criminal charges, and convictions or involvement in civil suits are public, but privacy laws protect most other personal information. Faith leaders may want to know but may *not* have a right to certain information that can only be released by an individual. Depending on state law, that information usually includes the following:

- Driving records
- Employment evaluations and references
- Credit reports
- Criminal complaints or allegations
- Hospitalization and/or reason for hospitalization

Bertha's reputation depended on the congregation viewing her as capable and invincible, so she told no one of her heart failure. She was horrified when her rabbi mentioned her hospitalization during worship and prayed for her recovery. Contrary to HIPAA (Health Insurance Portability and Accountability Act) guidelines, the rabbi received the information from a nurse in the congregation who worked at the hospital and simply assumed that Bertha would appreciate the prayer support. Bertha was hardly appreciative; she threatened to sue both the nurse and the rabbi.

Those with supervisory roles may have a right to know certain personal information about clergy and staff, but if and only if that information has a direct impact on the person's professional functioning and conduct. Supervisors may be senior staff and members of a personnel committee or another committee to which the supervisory responsibility for employees has been delegated. Contrary to the myths that congregational leaders have a right to know *everything* about their clergy, the personnel committee and others in supervisory roles only have a right to know about specifically job-related issues, such as Internet behavior on the job; sexual relationships that violate legal and religious codes of ethics; or alcohol, drug, or other addictions affecting professional performance and responsibilities.

Because of the First Amendment separation of church and state, religious groups can determine exactly whom they choose to ordain and what the criteria will be. They can ask many more questions during a clergy candidate's journey toward ordination than employers can legally ask of potential employees. Applicants for nonordained positions in a congregation can be asked about their faith; secular employers could be sued for asking such a question. Faith leaders should assume they have neither the right to know or to ask for personal information about their pastors, staff, or other congregational leaders—unless that personal issue directly affects job functioning and competence. Though the individual may willingly release the information if he or she chooses, the candidate cannot be coerced to offer information. Invasive questions that should be avoided include these topics:

- Family problems (with partner, children, and so forth)
- Psychological diagnoses or other mental challenges
- Whether the person is in the care of a mental-health specialist
- Medical condition
- Personal finances (wealth, indebtedness, money management)
- Prior victimization (from abuse, domestic violence, or other crime)
- Intimate relationships (dating, divorce, separation)
- Sexual orientation
- Sexual partners
- Questions about functioning related to gender

Though the information above may be personal, it is the clergyperson's ethical responsibility to identify any issues that might compromise job performance and to address those with supervision or remediation before they escalate. One rabbi suffering from multiple sclerosis refused to acknowledge his medical condition when he was first hired by his congregation. Over his years there, he suffered continuous criticism from congregants about his behavior and limitations, as if they were personality faults and not consequences of the progressing disease. Instead of gracefully retiring with a medical disability, he was forced to resign.

The issues in the list above relate to private information, but privacy for clergy is not easily confined to boundaries of time or place. A clergyperson is rarely off duty. When a police officer discovered that a pastor clandestinely met his sexual partners under a bridge, the officer laughingly told others in the police department about having to ask the pastor and his lover to leave. As the story spread within the department and then out into the community, the pastor's seemingly private behavior dramatically affected his credibility at church and his reputation in town.

An ethics code for ministry professionals states that ministry professionals "do not engage in conduct that compromises their professional responsibilities or reduces the public's trust in the profession."[1] When congregational leaders become concerned that an issue such as one of those on the list above may be affecting professional performance and effectiveness, they should carefully pursue their concerns.

The vestry worried that their rector, Kathy, showed up at the office later each morning and became suspicious that she might be hung over from partying the night before. At first her ministry did not appear to be impaired by this behavior, but the pattern continued for a couple of months. Nancy, a vestry member, asked Kathy over for lunch and in the privacy of her home chatted awhile, then cautious with her wording, compassionately asked Kathy, "How are things going?" Teary-eyed, Kathy confided that she was pregnant for the fourth time but had miscarried every other time. She physically felt terrible but was afraid to say anything to the vestry until she had passed her first trimester. Nancy promised to keep the information between the two of them until Kathy could share it herself when she chose to. Had Nancy been more specific in her question or chosen to tell the vestry about the pregnancy against Kathy's wishes, she not only would have jeopardized her relationship with Kathy but because she was a church official she also might have been accused of invading Kathy's privacy and meddling. Instead, she and Kathy agreed to a response Nancy could give if anyone asked what was wrong with Kathy. Nancy would say, "Our committee is aware of her schedule change. It's just temporary, and she's fine." Kathy was granted the privacy she needed, and confidence was built in the committee's oversight of the pastor's work responsibilities.

Need to Know

Just because someone has a right to know particular information does not necessarily mean he or she has a need to know. A dad with small children has both the right and the need to know about the risks posed by a neighbor rumored to be a child molester, and he can and should check the public registry of sex offenders. A pastor may hear gossip that a parishioner was charged with tax evasion 15 years earlier but has no need to verify the rumor by checking public records, unless the pastor wants to address the related church gossip or that parishioner volunteers to count the Sunday offering.

The need to know is less a legal concept than a subjective one, based on opinion about a specific situation or relationship. Matthew 18:15–17 is a scriptural example of the need-to-know concept, which restricts knowledge of an offense to the smallest number possible: "If another member of the church sins against you, go and point out the fault when the two of you are alone." First, no one needs to know of the offense except the two individuals involved. "But if you are not listened to, take one or two others along with you, so that every word may be confirmed by the evidence of two or three witnesses." If more people are needed to encourage reconciliation, the information circle widens to three or four. "If the member refuses to listen to them, tell it to the church." Finally, the need to know expands to the faith community because the problem behavior now affects them all.

According to pastoral counselor and educator Wendell Miller, "The circle of knowledge should be limited to those who are: (1) a part of the problem, (2) a part of the solution to the problem, and (3) affected by the problem."[2] Some information may be helpful but not vital to know. A clergyperson may gain a better understanding of a congregant's struggles if she knows more about the family's history. But she doesn't *need* to know that story to effectively minister to the congregant. The concept of needing to know relates to more crucial information necessary for adequate functioning or for the safety of an individual or organization. Attorneys describe need-to-know information on two levels, "demonstrated" or "compelling" levels, which are applicable to congregations. Certain individuals have a "demonstrated need to know" some information, because that information is necessary for the person to adequately function in his or her professional role. First-time visitors to a congregation need to know when weekly worship starts, otherwise they show up too late or too early. A congregation has a demonstrated need to know its own income and expense budget, otherwise it cannot wisely make decisions about its future. Certain individuals have a "compelling need to know" other information, because not knowing that information could result in some sort of harm. The congregation has a compelling need to know about past embezzlement when selecting its treasurer, who registered sex offenders are in the community, and past boundary crossings when hiring a pastor or rabbi.

When elected to chair the Safe Congregation committee, Jason became responsible for policies regarding drivers for youth field trips. Because the driving duties were infrequent, the volunteers weren't required to go through as thorough a screening as the youth advisors. At a minimum, Jason wanted to be sure that each driver

had current automobile insurance and a clean driving record. He
believed that for the safety of the young people, he had a compelling
need to know that information. But when he went to the Department of Motor Vehicles (DMV), he discovered that by state law,
individuals had to personally request their driving records.

Regardless of how crucial it was that Jason know that information, he had no right to access it. He asked his employer how she
got insurance and driving records for the delivery staff, and she
said every one of them was required to bring in a DMV report
annually, because even she as an employer couldn't access those
records directly. She had a need to know but no right to know. So
Jason developed a policy for the congregation that before driving
anyone other than one's own children on the youth field trips, a
driver had to supply the youth director with copies of a DMV
record and evidence of insurance coverage.

When Information Needs to Be Revealed

Sometimes clergy and lay leaders must reveal information to others
within the congregation or beyond it. Most professional organizations and religious judicatories require the release of information if
concealing it might result in harm to another person. The American Association of Pastoral Counselors (AAPC) allows release of
confidential client information "to prevent a clear and immediate
danger to someone." The American Psychological Association
(APA) used less restrictive wording "to protect the patient or client or others from harm," dropping the specificity of "clear and
immediate."[3] State statutes also require certain service providers to
report to civil authorities any reasonable suspicions of abuse against
children, youth, adults over 64, and adults who may be dependent
on others for their care. All clergy and lay leaders responsible for
the oversight of children should carefully check both state laws
and their judicatory guidelines for information that needs to be
reported to authorities. If the information concerns suspicions of

abusive behavior, state law may require that a report be made to law enforcement or other civil authorities, with or without the person's permission. In situations that do not legally mandate disclosure, faith leaders should obtain oral or written consent from any individual before sharing information related to that person.

Sometimes the need to open up old information isn't based on a legal mandate at all, but involves old secrets that need to become known and worked through for the overall health of a congregation. At the orientation for the newly hired youth director, the administrative pastor explained some of the congregation's policies for the safety and protection of youth. For example, youth advisors had to be no fewer than five years older than the oldest youth group participants and all drivers to events had to be twenty years or older with excellent driving records. Another rule was that no sofas were allowed in any offices. Though the senior staff had thought that the church had finally rid itself of all its past secrets, more than a year went by before one of the youth advisors had the courage to ask about the sofa rule, which he thought was strange. The advisors had never been told about the former youth pastor who had sexually abused youth group members, often taking advantage of them on the sofa in his office. Inadvertently, the secret had developed again and it needed to be disclosed once again.

At times information needs to be revealed when clergy need professional advice, consultation, or supervision. Sometimes a faith leader decides he or she simply must call the insurance agent or a lawyer for a consultation. As mentioned in an earlier chapter, in this professional conversation, leaders protect as many details as possible, sharing only what is absolutely necessary to gain the guidance needed. Leaders could follow the guidelines of the American Psychological Association (APA), which say, "When consulting with colleagues, (1) psychologists do not share confidential information that reasonably could lead to the identification of a patient, client, research participant, or other person or organization with whom they have a confidential relationship unless they have obtained the prior consent of the person or organization or the disclosure cannot be avoided, and (2) they share information only to the extent necessary to achieve the purposes of the consultation."[4]

Not Wanting to Know

Members and constituents in congregations have become less con-nected to their denominational roots. Our population is increasingly characterized by individualism, mobility, and interfaith marriage, and therefore more worshipers are switching from one denomina-tion to another.[5] As a result of this fluid denominational loyalty, today's congregation leaders may have little if any background or understanding of the organizational structure, rules, or traditions of the faith communities they lead. Religious judicatories, hoping to enhance denominational loyalty and knowledge, are increasingly articulating their doctrines in print, online, and in special leadership training sessions. Yet, with the wealth of publicly accessible infor-mation about individual faith traditions, surprisingly few congre-gational leaders have much knowledge about their denomination's polity or the authority and responsibility of their positions.

Congregational consultants have frequently had to teach leaders how their constitutions and bylaws work and the ins and outs of their particular governance. Concerned about this pattern, Kibbie Ruth interviewed elected faith leaders in 2001, asking if they thought it was necessary to know their denomination's polity and policies. Fewer than half said yes—even though their effective leadership depended on that knowledge. Having a *right* to know certain information and the obvious *need* to know it does not nec-essarily inspire an interest in that knowledge.

This hesitancy or refusal to know the policies and procedures of the denomination can inhibit congregational health. The lay people serving on the governing council of one congregation had no idea that with their election to office came the responsibility for making decisions about the activities, finances, and direction of their faith community. The council routinely rubber-stamped whatever the pastor said he wanted. When financial misappropriations, staff unrest, and harassment surfaced, the council initially just nodded through the pastor's explanation for why things weren't going well. More and more people left the church in discomfort over the cronyism that seemed to ignore legal liability. Then a new council member gave her colleagues a copy of the denomination's governing manual for local churches. The council was stunned to discover the authority and responsibility it had, and immediately began to reshape the congregational culture to give lay leaders the power that the denominational polity intended.

The hesitancy or refusal to make use of public and easily accessed information may also affect the safety of members of the congregation. The desire *not to know* may overcome the desire *to know*. One pastor complained, "If I find someone's name on the registry of sex offenders, then I'd have to do something about it. But if I don't know . . . well, that would just be easier."

What are the appropriate boundaries around information in congregations? Faith leaders answer this question most effectively by expanding the amount of information available to their congregations as broadly as possible to ensure transparency and the overall health of the body. However, the goal of transparency doesn't mean everyone knows everything about everybody. Leaders need to consider (1) who has a *right to know* what, (2) who has a *need to know* that information, and (3) what information should be disclosed because it is relevant or necessary to ensure the safety and well-being of the congregation. Particularly sensitive subjects require an additional understanding of legal issues and are discussed in the next chapter.

Chapter 7

Legal Issues

When facing disclosure questions in volatile situations, congregation leaders may be inclined to shut down the flow of information. When people are anxious, they are more likely to panic about potential lawsuits and to cover up necessary information by using legal terms and language. Too often a congregation shuts down communication with explanations such as, "It's confidential" or "We can't legally share that with you." Sometimes people make such statements to get their way in an argument, but most often people of good intentions are simply trying to protect their congregations and clergy from missteps that could lead to litigation.

Members of boards and committees tend to underdisclose information out of fear—"We'll get sued!" Yet many disclosures are crucial in order to make congregations safe from harassment and abuse, to screen out inappropriate candidates at the time of hiring, to inform judicatories of potentially harmful issues, and to allow for healing after a breach of trust has occurred.

On the other hand, some disclosures in congregations are made with little regard to the potential damage that could follow. Say a family in one congregation leaves and joins another congregation and their former pastor speaks negatively of them, using them as an example in a sermon. The congregation could be sued for slander if damages could be proven in court.

The complex legal issues surrounding communication may overwhelm congregation leaders. When the threat of a lawsuit arises in a congregation, state and federal laws and denominational guidelines may both apply, making disclosure dilemmas extremely complex. Although some lawsuits may not be successful, faith leaders should carefully consider how they manage information and openly address their questions about possible litigation. Religious bodies and congregations have no divine immunity, as is obvious from the deluge of suits surrounding clergy sexual abuse. As people learn more about personnel issues and ethics regarding disclosures in their workplaces, they bring new expectations to their congregations. Members have a growing awareness that if they are not dealt with fairly, they can sue. As one attorney wisely noted, "Anyone can sue anyone else for anything at any time."

If your congregation is having difficulty making decisions between openly telling the truth and protecting information out of fear of slandering someone, bring a clergy consultant or attorney into the dialogue. Attorneys with experience in congregational issues provide the best advice, because congregations are governed by their own rules as well as local, state, and federal laws. Having coexisting and frequently changing sets of religious and secular guidelines is confusing; therefore, for prudent decision making, leaders must understand the most up-to-date versions of all legal guidelines.

As mentioned above, in the current climate of increasing litigation by individuals and class-action groups, congregations are more likely to face lawsuits. Also, when a case involves a faith group, obtaining impartial legal decisions can be particularly difficult because jurors often have biases related to beliefs and to the institutions that promote them.[1] Rabbi and lawyer Arthur Schaefer puzzles over the reaction of clergy and religious organizations to increasingly successful lawsuits against them. He notes that they are either proactive or in denial. Some buy malpractice insurance, implement child protective policies, and reduce the extent of counseling performed by clergy. Others simply ignore the growing trend of litigation in hopes that it will never affect them.

To encourage proactive liability reduction, this chapter briefly describes general legal terms and issues related to disclosure of information by faith leaders. How much immunity and privilege can congregations expect to have? What religious and secular rules should faith leaders consider when deciding whether to disclose the information they inevitably receive? This is by no means an exhaustive analysis of the law or intended to act as or be a substitute for appropriate legal advice. However, armed with some basic information, clergy and lay members of congregations can identify potential areas of liability and exercise reason and common sense to avoid litigation.

Criminal or Civil?

Criminal cases involve individuals who are accused of violating certain legal statutes. An entity, such as a whole congregation, usually cannot be charged with a criminal act, although the directors, trustees, and other "agents" who lead that entity can be. For example, a congregation cannot *itself* be charged with committing the crime of child sexual abuse in its preschool; however, *individuals* who are members, constituents, employees, or volunteers of the preschool are criminally liable for their own wrongful acts and therefore can be prosecuted and punished.

A whole congregation as an institution can find itself liable for intentional or unintentional harm caused to others. Those cases are filed in civil court and may result in monetary awards. Most complaints against congregations involve "torts"—the concept that injury to a person or to property should be compensated. Torts include such wrongdoings as the infliction of mental distress, defamation, and invasion of privacy. Negligence is an additional tort regarding breach of duty that results in harm to another, such as failure to provide sufficient oversight for a program or activity.

Two congregations learned the difference between criminal and civil cases in two situations involving members' personal information. One church eagerly adopted a new contribution system so that donors could use their credit cards to pay their pledges, but leaders failed to put proper safeguards in place, and donor credit information was disclosed to a number of key leaders on the finance committee. Not long thereafter, the assistant treasurer was arrested for grand theft for using a member's credit card information for personal purchases. While the offending assistant treasurer was appearing in criminal court, the church leaders were in civil court defending themselves and the congregation itself from charges of the negligent disclosure of personal information and a potentially expensive settlement.

A similar case involved a synagogue that failed to protect the Social Security numbers they required on volunteer screening applications. When one of those numbers was used in an identity theft, the office volunteer who had photocopied them faced criminal charges, and the synagogue faced a civil suit to recover the financial losses the members had suffered. In both cases, better information management would have saved the congregations from such painful lessons in legal responsibility and legal consequences.

First Amendment Protections

Many congregations assume that the First Amendment to the U.S. Constitution, which provides for the separation of church and state, protects them from legal liability, but this is not always so. The First Amendment prohibits the government from advancing a particular religion or inhibiting anyone's religious belief,[2] which means the government can neither do anything to establish or promote a particular religion nor regulate anyone's religious belief. Additionally, the First Amendment prohibits civil courts from deciding religious, denominational, or doctrinal disputes. For example, the civil courts cannot determine the "minimal standards of training or education that clergy or lay people need."[3]

Courts have determined that "[t]he First Amendment absolutely protects the freedom to believe, but conduct, even when religiously motivated, is not totally free of government regulation."[4] Religious organizations can be sued for some of their activities in the secular world. Faith leaders cannot "under the banner of the First Amendment provisions on religion . . . with impunity defame a person, intentionally inflict serious emotional harm on a parishioner, or commit other torts."[5] The state can require congregations to comply with laws that are neutral, such as mandated reporting of child abuse and building codes, and that do not interfere, directly or indirectly, with the exercise of a sincerely held religious belief. In their verbal or written disclosure of information, faith leaders risk difficulties if they act outside either the established patterns of their denomination's practices[6] or the legal codes of the state.

Clergy Malpractice

Many an aggrieved party threatens to sue a minister and congregation for clergy malpractice, and congregations usually purchase clergy malpractice insurance to protect themselves. However, most clergy malpractice complaints "are dismissed quickly, lost at trial or thrown out on appeal."[7] Still, clergy malpractice insurance is required by most package insurance programs for congregations. Wisconsin-based Church Mutual Insurance Company first introduced clergy malpractice insurance in 1968[8]—even though the malpractice tort for clergy did not exist at that time.[9] Until 1980 no insurance company ever paid a claim on such a policy. In spite of their failure in court, however, since the 1980 case hundreds of lawsuits have included the claim of malpractice in hopes of a financial settlement. Many of these lawsuits do succeed under other legal definitions.

What happened in 1980? The family of a young man sued Grace Community Church of the Valley in Sun Valley, California, and its pastors because their pastoral care allegedly failed to prevent the young man's suicide.[10] It was the first lawsuit in the United States in which clergy malpractice was alleged as a separate cause of action, even though the decision was later withdrawn by order of the Supreme Court of California. Although several courts have since been confronted with the question whether clergy malpractice constitutes a separate, recognizable cause of legal action, no case has yet recognized it as such.[11]

According to church legal specialist Richard Hammar, the claim of clergy malpractice is difficult to prove because

> such a claim requires definition of relevant standard of care. Defining that standard could embroil courts in establishing the training, skill, and standards applicable for members of the clergy in a diversity of religions with widely varying beliefs. Furthermore, defining such a standard would require courts to identify the beliefs and practices of the relevant religion and then to determine whether the clergy had acted in accordance with them. The entanglement could restrain the free exercise of religion.[12]

Therefore, lawyers usually change the complaints of clergy malpractice to "breach of fiduciary duty," because that claim does not require first establishing a standard of care and then a violation of that standard. Breach of fiduciary duty only requires the proof that an understood trust in a relationship was violated. A complaint of breach of fiduciary duty, however, usually results in an unsuccessful claim, because it requires clarification of a clergyperson's duty and therefore would entangle courts with free exercise of religion.[13]

Fiduciary Duty

Clergy and congregations have a moral, ethical, and potentially a legal obligation to disclose information in a way that protects individuals within the organization from harm. The accepted definition of *fiduciary duty* is based on the legal comments in a 1997

New Jersey case against a clergyperson.[14] In a fiduciary relationship between a clergyperson and a congregant or counselee, the clergy is in a dominant or superior position and owes a "duty of care" to the person who has placed trust and confidence in him or her. This duty includes exercise of reasonable skill while acting for or giving advice for the benefit of another person on matters within the scope of their relationship. Accordingly, clergy could be liable for harm resulting from a breach of those duties if the person is harmed or injured in some way and the breach of duty "proximately" caused the injury for which damages are sought.[15]

This definition describes well why clergy should not misuse the pastoral relationship for personal gain—why they should not accept financial favors, sexualize the relationship, or use personal power to manipulate, harass, or demean others. Clergy must morally use the duty of care with information that is given to them in trust. But because the First Amendment limits the court's ability to define the pastoral role, complaints of breach of fiduciary duty continue to fail in court.[16]

One such case began this way. A pastor on an outreach visit dropped by the Hesters' home and explained that he was an ordained minister in the area. During their conversation, he encouraged them to trust and confide in him, promising them confidentiality. Instead, he later told many others about the family's personal life, including untrue allegations. When the Hesters sued, the court stated that the "tradition that a spiritual advisor does not divulge communications received in that capacity ... describes a moral, not a legal duty. In the absence of a legal duty, a breach of a moral duty does not suffice to invest tort liability."[17] Put more simply, the courts could not define his fiduciary duty as a pastor without interfering in the religious tradition of his faith, so the Hesters did not win on that point. The pastor was not off the hook, however. In this case, like most others, charges were filed under several legal categories and while failing under one, they succeeded under others. The Hesters' attorneys were able to win substantial awards for the couple under the legal categories of defamation of character and invasion of privacy.

Common Legal Actions against Congregations

Common legal actions related to poor information management by faith leaders may include negligence, defamation of character, infliction of emotional distress, and invasion of privacy. Both congregational leaders and the congregation as an institution can be liable for monetary damages. The specific grounds for these legal actions differ by state; therefore, seeking legal assistance from someone who knows statutory law, case law (similar cases that have been won and lost), and relevant denominational policies is prudent.

Negligence

Most claims against congregations involve cases of negligence. Negligence can be established when a person who has a legal duty toward another person unintentionally breaches or fails to perform that duty and, as a result, the other person is harmed in a manner that could have been foreseen. For example, the congregation owes a duty to those who come into its building to be sure that the building is safe. If some condition makes the building unsafe, the congregation has the duty to warn those who enter. If a custodian does not tell others that he has just mopped the floor and someone falls on the slippery surface and breaks a leg, his failure to warn, or to disclose, the safety-related information about the wet floor could result in the congregation's being sued for negligence because of the injury.

Three components define negligence: (1) The person or organization had a legal duty toward the other person, (2) the person or organization unintentionally breached or failed to perform that duty, and as a result, (3) the other person is harmed in a manner that could have been foreseen.

If a church staff person is aware that one of the regular worshipers is a convicted registered sex offender, is there a duty to warn other worshipers? Certainly the sex offender's presence presents a risk just like the slippery floor. If a staff member who knew this information chose not to inform the church members and a member was abused by the offender, then all three components of negligence would exist. The church could be held financially responsible in civil court for any resulting injuries. A better approach would be to have the staff or the sex offender disclose that fact to the congregation in such a way that the risk would be greatly reduced.

In a recent negligence case, a Seventh Day Adventist conference was ordered to pay two million dollars in damages to the victim of sexual abuse perpetrated by the son of a church's pastor.[18] In that case, the pastor had been reassigned from Washington to Oregon after both the pastor and his supervisor became aware that the pastor's eleven-year-old son had engaged in sexual activity with at least one girl in the Washington parish. They kept that activity secret from the elders and everyone else at the Oregon church, in spite of the risk the son posed to other children. When the preteen molested a five-year-old girl at the new church, the court found the Adventist conference, as the pastor's employer, to have breached its duty—a duty to warn the elders of the Oregon church of the risk the boy posed and to require the pastor to supervise his son when the son accompanied him during pastoral activities. Had the Oregon congregation known the information and failed to share it and protect its children, it also could have been sued. Even though the conference in this situation had no right to control the conduct of the eleven-year-old, the court clearly recognized the duty a religious body has to warn its congregants of a known risk of harm. Information must be carefully disclosed if failure to do so puts any member of the congregation at risk.

Defamation

Just as the Hebrew and Christian scriptures condemn verbally hurting anyone, civil laws also forbid publicly defaming another's character. A defamatory communication tends to harm the reputation of another—that is, lowers him or her in the estimation of the community or deters third persons from associating or dealing with him or her.[19] The comments may result in a person being hated, held in contempt, ridiculed, shunned, or losing the goodwill, confidence, and respect of the community.[20] This "offense of injuring a person's character, fame or reputation by false and malicious statements"[21] usually exceeds common gossip between individuals. But sometimes even "innocent" gossip can create injury. Say, for example, a congregation member spread the story that his minister had recently won the lottery and included the suggestion that she has a gambling addiction. The minister might have grounds for a defamation case if the rumor damaged her reputation or limited her ability to effectively do ministry in the community.

To effectively govern their congregations, faith leaders must deal with lots of uncomfortable, "negative" information—everything from the behavior of difficult parishioners to shortfalls in the budget because of overspending by a staff member. The law provides certain protections that allow for the reasonable and necessary flow of information in congregations. Statements made in the public interest, such as the statutorily mandated reporting of child abuse, generally cannot be the basis of a suit for defamation—so long as the report was made in good faith, and without malice.

However, disclosure can result in liability for defamation when the following occurs: (1) a false or defamatory statement must have been made about the person, (2) unprivileged communication of the statement must have been disseminated orally or in writing to another person, and (3) the statement must have resulted in economic damage to the person or be *actionable per se*.

In some situations of libel (defamation in writing) and slander (spoken defamation), damages do not have to be spelled out for a case to be won but are assumed to be damaging by the nature of the disclosures themselves. These cases may be "actionable per se." Derived from a Latin phrase meaning "through itself," *per se* means that the plaintiff does not need to prove any injurious effect caused by the statement, because the statement itself is in its very nature defamatory. Statements that are actionable per se include accusations that the person committed a serious crime; assertions that someone has a communicable or loathsome disease; false accusations of misconduct or dishonesty in the person's profession or employment; or derogatory statements about someone's business, trade, or profession.[22] The court assumes that a statement of this type will "through itself" injure the reputation of the person; therefore it does not require the plaintiff to show that his or her reputation has actually been diminished in the community or that economic loss has been suffered as a result of the statement.

A common saying in defamation cases is that the truth is an absolute defense. However, the "truth" may be more difficult to prove in court than the speaker or writer believes at the time of the statement.[23] The person being sued for defamation must establish the truth of what was written or said. In addition, although the facts related in the statement may be true, the implication of the statement may be defamatory. The classic example is the statement that a person is no longer beating his wife. Truth it may be, but the implication is that he had committed a crime before. So faith leaders should be cautious about the accuracy of any personal information they release.

In general, the law imposes a duty on everyone to behave at least as carefully as a reasonable person would in a similar situation, acting in good faith by disclosing information only to those who have a right and a need to know it. That is, one person who has an interest in the subject matter may disclose to another who also has an interest in it. The legal concept of the "common interest privilege" provides some leeway in the use of information within organizations. It allows for the free exchange of relevant information among those engaged in a "common enterprise" and permits them to make appropriate internal communications and share consultations. Operating under the common interest privilege, congregations can disclose information in order to meet their fiduciary duty (to protect) while reducing the likelihood of being sued.

Disclosures among pastor, elders, governing boards, and staff are usually protected by the common interest privilege, unless a statement is made maliciously or with knowledge of its falsity or reckless disregard for whether it is true. So congregations need to look to the purpose for which the statement is made and the manner in which it is made—why, how, and to whom it is communicated.

Discretion in disclosure is essential. If the church secretary sees the youth pastor viewing child-pornography Web sites, she may share that information with the pastor under the common interest privilege. Her comments may be defamatory if she shares the same information in a social gathering, especially if the church secretary was not actually sure that the youth pastor was viewing child pornography or if she fabricated the facts. The pastor should disclose the allegation only to those who have an identified responsibility for such information. The personnel committee, for example, may need to disclose the nature of the allegation and discuss the matter at its meeting in order to determine whether the youth pastor, by virtue of this alleged incident, presents a risk of harm to youth in the church.

What kinds of disclosures *would likely* lead to costly litigation? In one lawsuit, when a rector wrote in the church newsletter about the church secretary's firing, he opined that she was maliciously trying to discredit him. The court ruled that even though he said "in my opinion," it did not lessen his defamation of the woman.[24] If he had shared his opinion with his supervisor or the personnel committee prior to her firing, his statements might not have been the basis for a claim for damages. When he spoke out in the church newsletter, however, no one could argue that every recipient of that publication had a common interest in the information or needed to know his opinion. Other litigation resulted from a situation in which letters were written by one minister accusing another minister of "stealing, failing to pay debts, and carrying out 'Satan's plan' of dividing churches."[25] When one's honesty, trustworthiness, or morality is impugned, his or her reputation is almost certainly damaged.[26] Such defamation suits can be successfully litigated and can cost congregations their own reputations as well as large sums of money.

The apostle Paul directed his young fellow ministers Timothy and Titus to let their exemplary speech reflect the purity and soundness of their faith and actions (1 Tim. 4:12; Titus 2:7–8).[27] Faith leaders should do likewise in their communications:

- In general, speak well of others. Do not communicate with a spirit of anger, vindictiveness, or malice.
- Limit sensitive information to those who have a right and a need to know, that is, only "duly responsible"[28] parties with a legitimate reason for hearing the statement.
- When having to share volatile or potentially damaging information with others, stick to facts without commentary.
- Be cautious that what is spoken in meetings and worship or published in congregational materials is accurate and verifiable in both fact and implication.
- If defamatory remarks are made, retract them immediately.

These precautions will reduce the possibility of defamation lawsuits as well as increase the overall health of congregational communication.

Infliction of Emotional Distress

Stories of lawsuits so permeate the media that people often assume they can receive money anytime they suffer emotional pain or discomfort. If they can blame their pain or discomfort on an organization, they may in fact file a lawsuit to receive compensation. The law, however, does not protect individuals from any and all distress.

The law recognizes actual mental injury caused by anyone with *intent* to inflict emotional distress. The conduct complained of must be so outrageous and extreme that it cannot be tolerated in civilized society. Often these legal complaints contain words describing the defendant's action as "outrageous" or "far beyond the pale of expected human behavior."[29] Some courts add the element of a "willful, wanton, and reckless disregard of the consequences where there is a high probability that harm will occur."[30] As it relates to extreme situations of disclosure or concealment of information in the congregation, this claim rarely stands alone but usually accompanies a defamation, sexual harassment, negligence, or other claim for liability.

Invasion of Privacy

Often lawsuits alleging defamation and the intentional infliction of emotional distress include claims regarding invasions of privacy. Although the U.S. Constitution contains no protection of one's privacy,[31] over time individual states have created right of privacy protections based on the concept that a person is entitled to keep thoughts, feelings, or self-knowledge private. Congregations have a legal and an ethical obligation to respect individual privacy. Personal information is private property; therefore, only the person to whom it belongs should determine when, how, and with whom it may be disclosed.

Of the four invasion of privacy categories[32] outlined by tort scholar William Prosser,[33] the two forms of invasion of privacy most relevant to information management in a congregation are (1) placing someone in a false light, even with truthful information,[34] and (2) the publication of true, private facts that common law regards as essentially nobody's business.[35] In these cases, the truth of the information disclosed does not matter, because the basis for the claim is the disclosure itself rather than the defamatory nature of the disclosure. So even when information is factually true and positive in nature, faith leaders must exercise caution in disclosing private facts about members of their congregations or other colleagues.

To successfully claim invasion of privacy in either category, a person must show that private facts about him or her were disseminated to the public at-large or to so many people that the information is substantially certain to become public knowledge. In other words, the information was released without a "legitimate concern"—that is, a need to know. Also, the disclosure of this information must be considered highly offensive to a reasonable person.[36] The risk of invading someone's privacy is usually reduced when facts are obtained from independent and clearly nonconfidential sources.[37]

Claims of invasion of privacy by a clergyperson, congregation, or religious group have included cases such as "pulpit denunciations, disclosed confessions, [and] harsh indoctrination procedures . . . inducing the disclosure of privileged communications, employment discrimination, interference with marital and family relationships, and shunning."[38] Occasionally a congregation has been sued for information that was spread among leaders and congregants about sexual orientation,[39] adultery,[40] or other sexual behavior. Even if comments about sexual orientation or behavior are true, their publication could be claimed to invade privacy and damage someone's reputation.

An uneasy tension exists between the public interest and the right to be left alone. So if a church newsletter publishes personal information about a member that results in serious harm, the church may be liable. For example, a victim of domestic violence fled her home and moved to another town to escape her abusive partner. When her former congregation naively published her address change in the newsletter, a lawsuit could have resulted if the abuser used that information, tracked her down, and seriously assaulted her once more.

Even though congregations routinely publish addresses and phone numbers or pray for those in the hospital, no congregation should use someone's personal data without that person's permission.

The federally mandated HIPAA (Health Insurance Portability and Accountability Act) privacy rules do not apply to congregations but exemplify the caution with which the rest of society discloses an individual's information. Congregations should protect personal information, including medical or psychological conditions, matters of sexual orientation, and marital or financial problems a member may be experiencing. If it is impossible to obtain a person's consent, congregational leaders need to use ordinary care and common sense and consider how the disclosure of such information about someone might affect that person. If the disclosure is not offensive to a reasonable person, liability for sharing the information is unlikely.

Sensitive information is particularly problematic. A youth pastor discovered information in the church secretary's desk that he believed established that she and the senior pastor were sexually involved. After disclosing the information along with his suspicions of the affair to many people in the congregation, he was asked by the senior pastor to recant his story. Following a church-sanctioned healing process, he apologized for the pain he had caused and agreed to keep silent. But he did not. Soon all the church members knew about the alleged affair; many began calling for the dismissal of the secretary, and the church fired her. She was scorned by her community and was unable to obtain subsequent employment. The secretary sued the youth pastor and the church for defamation and invasion of privacy. The church was ordered to pay compensatory and punitive damages not only for disclosing her information from private files but also for the manner in which the information was disclosed.[42]

Again, the issue of what information is disclosed and how it is done becomes key. If the youth pastor had simply shared the information with the church staff and administration, the common interest privilege mentioned above in the defamation section might preclude legal action. However, he told others and the church ultimately believed his rumors of sexual misconduct and eventually ratified his repeating of those rumors by dismissing the secretary. Considering the large award for punitive damages in this case, congregational leaders must recognize and respect the privacy of the information for which they become responsible and limit its dissemination.

Clergy Privilege

One pastor intimidated his parishioners by loosely using legal language they did not understand. When church leaders raised concerns about his behavior, he often avoided addressing their concerns with the explanation, "I don't need to respond to that, because of clergy privilege." An elder finally asked a lawyer to explain the term and as a result realized the pastor was using the term to avoid accountability. "Clergy privilege" does not apply to information withheld from the congregation or its leaders but what can be withheld from court testimony.

From a legal perspective, the general term *privilege* "is an immunity or exemption from a duty (or requirement) that would otherwise bind a person."[43] One type of legal privilege is called clergy privilege or clergy-penitent privilege. This privilege exempts clergy from testifying in a court of law in certain circumstances. It honors the restrictions in denominational policies that prevent clergy from repeating certain information and gives clergy the right to withhold from the court information gained in penitential communication. If the confessing parishioner "waives the privilege" by giving the clergyperson permission to disclose previously confidential information, then no legal impediment keeps the clergyperson from testifying in court. Yet denominational rules for the clergyperson may still prohibit such testimony.

Though details of the privilege vary from state to state,[44] in general, the privilege can be claimed by clergy only when the communication is

- made privately and not in the presence of others
- not intended for further disclosure to others
- made to a member of the clergy, as defined by that faith group
- made while that clergyperson is acting in his or her official, professional capacity as a spiritual advisor

Not many communications qualify under these terms. Courts may rule that the communications were not penitential, as defined by the person's religious body or discipline. Courts may also determine that the definition of clergyperson does not include a lay pastor, a youth leader, or an individual who is not officially ordained. Some courts may decide that the communication occurred when the clergyperson was not acting in a professional capacity. Some courts have determined that clergy privilege does not apply when the penitent is not a member of the congregation, when more than one person is present when the clergyperson hears the information, or when the clergyperson is providing counseling rather than pastoral care. In some circumstances, the clergyperson is "obliged to testify as to observations made at the time even if not to the content of the confidential communication."[45]

When a California woman sued her Episcopal priest and other church officials for invasion of privacy and intentional infliction of emotional distress, she lost her arguments in court. When she told the rector about embezzling $28,000 from the church, she seemed to believe that her private communication was protected by something she had heard about confidentiality or clergy privilege. But the rector recognized that she was not confessing, certainly not as defined by his denomination; instead, she was trying to solve a problem before her improper accounting for the church was discovered. He called the police, and she was later convicted of grand larceny.[46] The rector testified in criminal court because the definition of clergy privilege did not apply to this situation. The civil court dismissed the woman's claim that her communication with him was private and therefore he should not have reported her to the police or been allowed to testify.

Neither clergy nor congregants can presume legal protection from a vaguely understood notion of "privilege." If called to testify, clergy need to be particularly savvy about both the tradition of their own religious group and their state's evidence code about clergy privilege. Confessions made to clergy have historically been respected as private and not subject to disclosure in court, even if the information contained in those confessions would sway the outcome in a trial. The governing rules of many faiths protect the confidences received by clergy; they define what can be disclosed and what must never be repeated. For example, the Book of Discipline for the United Methodist Church states that all clergy "are charged to maintain all confidences inviolate, including confessional confidences."[47] This statement was modified at the 2004 General Conference with the addition of these words, "except in the cases of suspected child abuse or neglect or in cases where mandatory reporting is required by civil law."

Many Protestant and Jewish clergy will find that few, if any, communications legally qualify under the term *religious privilege*, because their tradition has no regular practice of confessional or penitential communication. For example, most states' mandated child-abuse reporting laws[48] have complicated what is recognized as the clergy-penitent privilege. In fact, as of 2005, five states have denied *any* clergy-penitent privilege in child abuse cases regardless of the clergyperson's denominational confidentiality rules.[49]

Because the clergy-penitent privilege is related to disclosure in court proceedings, it does not apply to day-to-day functioning in the congregation. Few disclosures faith leaders receive in connection with their pastoral duties would fall under the clergy-penitent privilege. This is not to suggest that clergy should not honor their ethical responsibilities to maintain confidences. Rather it is to say that clergy cannot rely on the existence of this evidentiary privilege to justify concealing information.

Let's consider another situation that could arise in a congregation. When Mr. Alexander went to Rev. Culp for marital counseling, Rev. Culp assured him that anything he said to her in the session would be kept confidential. Mr. Alexander admitted to having several affairs during his marriage, including a current one. Shortly afterwards Rev. Culp met with Mr. Alexander's wife for lunch and not only disclosed the information she had agreed to keep confidential but also told the wife that her husband was a liar. She advised her to change the locks on the marital home, clean out the joint bank account, and seek a restraining order and a divorce. In addition, Rev. Culp disclosed the affair to a relative of the wife at a family gathering that same day.[50]

In this case, the husband sued both the minister and the church. The trial court dismissed the case, but the appellant court analyzed whether or not a violation of the clergy-penitent privilege had occurred. The husband claimed that privilege was a statement of a duty the minister owed him under the clergy-penitent statute. However, the court pointed out that the statute only prohibited clergy from disclosing the information in court proceedings and that the legislature had not intended to protect people from disclosure of confidential information outside legal proceedings.[51]

When dealing with sensitive information, faith leaders must be meticulous about following the regular and official policies and procedures within their congregation and religious tradition and carefully limiting information to those who have a need and a right to know. As long as the information is treated in a way that does not border on defamation, negligence, or invasion of privacy, clergy are free to make use of information for the greater good of the congregation.

Concluding Cautions

At a recent workshop on congregations at risk, a participant cornered the speaker during the break. "You're making us really anxious today," she said. "The more I know, the more I know that I need to know!" The purpose of this book is not to create anxiety, but raising anxiety may be worthwhile if that motivates individuals and congregations to implement protections against damage and resulting lawsuits.

Congregational polices that outline communication flow and responsibilities can protect confidential issues as well as increase the transparency of other information. In extremely stressful situations where the potential for lawsuits is high, grievance procedures, in particular, help tremendously. Rather than sitting on a library shelf, these information management policies need to become part of new member orientation and regularly disseminated to current members.

The value of consultation cannot be stressed enough when decisions about disclosures need to be made. Anxiety may alert leaders to increase protection; to seek professional advice; and to create, review, or implement policies. When a crisis challenges the congregation, leaders who have been conscientious about following their local church policies, denominational guidelines, and state laws will already have reduced the risk of liability in the congregation. A congregation free of litigation can live out its mission with joy.

Chapter 8

Leaders "In the Know"

The context of congregational life complicates any decision process. In congregations, individuals gather, each bringing his or her own history, emotions, and needs. The work of becoming a community includes the challenges inherent in a mixture of personalities, needs, and stories. To manage information in the midst of this complexity, discernment and wisdom require knowing ourselves, our roles, and our congregations. Leaders must be self-aware, educated about congregational and denominational polity, familiar with applicable civil laws, and aware of their congregation's core values and systemic dynamics. Leaders need to be "in the know" about these crucial basics, or the decisions they make about information may be ill advised. The greater congregational leaders' knowledge before making decisions, the better those decisions will be.

Father Joseph wanted to immediately send letters to his entire congregation when two teenaged boys told him that the youth group's adult sponsor had molested them. He quickly recognized, however, that such a mass mailing could trigger hysteria in the church and in the local press and community. Instead, Joseph calmed his racing mind and considered what to do with this information. After filing a child abuse report to police, as he was required to do by state law, Joseph later met with the detectives investigating the case. Though he was morally drawn to siding with all victims, Joseph tried to keep an open attitude. He soon learned from the detectives that the youth group's adult sponsor had recently talked to the parents of the alleged victims about what seemed to be alcohol on the breath of the boys when they came to youth group. The two teenagers were furious about what they perceived as a betrayal by the sponsor and were determined to get back at him. The story the detectives uncovered was substantiated by the parents, other youth group members they interviewed, and ultimately by the teen accusers themselves. Instead of accusing the adult sponsor in a letter to the whole congregation, Joseph offered pastoral care to the teenagers, their parents, and the adult sponsor. Information sharing was kept at a minimum—and the youth received professional help with their problem drinking. Had Father Joseph acted too quickly, healing the individuals and the congregation would have been nearly impossible.

To be prepared make prudent decisions, wise leaders need to know

- their own motivations and needs
- their role in the congregation and the congregation's polity
- ethical and legal standards of practice
- the beliefs and the core values of the congregation
- the systemic dynamics within the congregation itself

Know Yourself: Motivations and Needs

How a leader handles sensitive information depends on various personal characteristics, such as emotions, hopes, tacit expectations, old wounds, and family patterns. The background a faith leader brings to information management dilemmas affects the decisions made. Reflecting on a series of self-check questions can increase self-awareness.

How Am I Doing?

- Am I conscientious about my health and self-care?
- Are my personal and intimate relationships strong?
- Is my spiritual life thriving? Am I taking time for prayer and reflection?
- In my leadership role, am I aware of spiritual values upon which I make my decisions?

What Am I Up To?

- Whose needs am I trying to meet? Am I leading to pursue my own agenda or for the betterment of the congregation?
- Am I using individuals over whom I have authority to meet my personal needs?
- Can I live up to the expectations of character and behavior that come with my leadership position?
- Do I understand that simply because of my role in the church, other members may hear me differently, put more weight on my opinions, and be more easily influenced by me?
- How do I handle the power inherent in my position?

What Personal Issues Might Interfere with My Judgment?

- What opinions, attitudes, ideals, prejudices, and beliefs are reactive?
- What personal needs might get in the way (such as a desire to be liked, need for praise, wanting to avoid conflict and accountability, desire to know everything, or need for emotional safety)?
- Does this situation remind me of old family dynamics and vulnerabilities?
- How do I communicate and what are my ingrained, unconscious communication patterns? Do I evade

appropriate truth telling? Do I keep secrets, enjoy gossip, or spread rumors? Do I triangulate or use others to carry my message?

Personal issues affect the clarity of leaders' discernment and decision making. Addressing any issue through counseling, coaching, spiritual direction, or recovery practices helps leaders stay personally well-grounded, especially when their lives are rocked by changes or challenges.

When decisions related to concealing or revealing sensitive or volatile information must be made in a highly charged environment, wise discernment requires even greater self-awareness and spiritual centeredness. Some particularly volatile information stirs up intense anxiety within leaders and furor among congregants. The difficulty of a subject can push even the most self-aware leaders into denial and propel them into reactionary decisions. Leaders would be wise to take a deep breath, calm their anxiety, broaden their perspective, and deepen their spiritual grounding.

One church's governing body was savvy, healthy, and usually adept in their leadership roles, but in one situation they simply became stumped. A parishioner was repeatedly spreading slanderous rumors about the pastor. Every disclosure option the elected leaders discussed could potentially make the situation worse and even invite threats of lawsuits. Finally, the chairperson simply stopped the meeting for a 10-minute break for silence and prayer. The leaders wandered around the building for those 10 minutes "listening for the voice of God." When the group reconvened, one man excitedly said, "You know, when we stopped to really think about what this church values, our faith and our community, the right choice became so clear!" What he heard from God was to check the bylaws, of all things. There in print right under their noses were the pieces of information that helped the leaders design an appropriate and effective response that worked beautifully. The bylaws gave them permission to hold members accountable for their behavior and to ask them to resign from membership if their behavior continued to damage the worship life of the church. Their pause for deeper reflection opened their hearts and minds to wiser discernment.

Know Your Role

Understanding specific governing guidelines, leaders can serve effectively. The church mentioned above was dealing with someone trying to sabotage the pastor by claiming that he had acted seductively toward her. Witnesses of the alleged sexual advance discounted her claims, which appeared to be more about her dissatisfaction with church life and frustration with the pastor. Over the years her pattern of vicious and relentless criticism included everything from the length of the worship service to what was posted on bulletin boards in the hallways. Relying on denominational guidelines, leaders referred the allegation to their regional officials, who found no wrongdoing. Relying on their own church's bylaws, they found a clear, legal, and compassionate procedure implemented over several months to remove the woman from membership. Their decision making was easier because they knew their role as leaders and acted according to the local, regional, and national guidelines that applied to them and their church.

By contrast, some leaders exceed the boundaries of their responsibilities and influence decisions beyond their leadership realm. For example, an elder went behind the backs of the building renewal committee and dealt with the city planning department himself, not once but three times, before the committee realized what was creating so much delay in the approval of their remodeling plans. The committee then faced not only mending relationships with the planning department but also dismissing the elder from leadership on the committee for his lack of accountability to the process the group had established.

Clear job descriptions and accountability are key. Failure of leaders to effectively fulfill their governing responsibilities sometimes leaves voids that meddlesome parishioners fill. Some leaders stick their heads in the sand to avoid conflict or accountability and allow others to step into their roles, an easy move for the others to make when they have unofficial power that has never been questioned. Some leaders elected to represent and lead the congregation renege on their responsibility and let the clergy do all the governing. Clergy may dodge their responsibility by passing it to those who have greater authority, such as bishops and other judicatory leaders. Those authority figures may also avoid handling crises or conflicts because they are hesitant to accept the power of their office, and yet their assertive, legitimate leadership is crucial. When leaders fully know, understand, and exercise their roles and responsibilities, wiser decisions can be made and effective action taken.

Congregations are finding that special training sessions and denominational resources help bring new leaders up to speed and educate them on their roles and responsibilities, as well as consequences of behaving outside the boundaries of that role. The information in print and in the training includes denominational rules and polity; ethical standards, bylaws and other congregational policies; organizational charts; descriptions of committee membership and responsibility; job descriptions; and communication "road maps."

Leaders also need to know information about appropriate financial practices (including insurance coverage) and legal requirements, particularly related to employment law, harassment prevention, and abuse reporting. These resources, which equip laity and clergy for successful leadership, are available from their judicatories, the Alban Institute and other publishing houses, and online from various congregational consultants.

Know Your Congregation

Congregations, like other organizations and companies, need to make management decisions with their overall mission in mind.

Otherwise leaders tend toward maintenance of the status quo, expediency, or tunnel vision instead of seeing the bigger picture: what the congregation is called to be and do in the world. So healthy congregations prepare their leaders for wise decision making by articulating their theology and defining their mission and values.

Too often, however, congregations fail to identify their values or lay out a road map that takes them into the future. A crisis is hardly the time for an in-depth analysis of a congregation's foundational principles, and unfortunately major decisions often need to be made quickly and in the midst of tension. If a congregation has already laid the foundation by clarifying beliefs and values, it can revisit those values in times of crisis. Pausing, even in the midst of a highly stressful situation, is still advisable. Holding brief conversations about congregational values and vision is a way to establish priorities in the decision making that lies ahead.

Leaders can ask questions such as these:

- What is most important to us?
- On what principles are we grounded?[1]
- Where do we want to go in the future?

What congregations may proclaim in a mission statement may be quite different, however, from the core values and assumptions of individual leaders, the governing board, and the congregation itself. The direction and principles articulated by leaders may be trumped by longtime systemic dynamics in the congregation that more accurately define how and why things are done. Certain members may control the life of the congregation because they give the most, know the secrets, manipulate decisions, or simply have commanded the power for decades. Understanding the tacit dynamics in a congregation helps its leaders navigate the hidden landmines and establish boundaries, while they address damaging patterns within the faith community.[2]

When Laura attended worship services, she sensed an unexplainable edginess. She heard sermons that lifted up values such as forgiveness, accountability, loving one another, and being one in the body of Christ, as if these values were shared throughout the congregation and guided the church's leadership. But soon after she was elected to the governing board, she discovered something different. The conflict between the senior and associate pastors had grown in such intensity that the board called it "the pastoral war." What actually operated in the church was cheap grace rather than forgiveness, secrecy rather than appropriate confidentiality and transparency, and "niceness" and looking the other way rather than accountability. When the pastors' conflict exploded into legal threats against one another, Laura insisted the governing board hire a consultant to assist with the response and healing process. The consultant's strategy exposed the incongruence between expressed values and the actual practice, and she encouraged church leaders to reexamine the church's foundational principles and to think about where they had slipped off those foundations.

The congregation's tendency to avoid tension with the senior pastor had evolved into giving her complete control of almost every decision concerning the church. In their embarrassment about their lack of integrity and being elected to lead the congregation but failing to do so, members of the governing board had, over time, increasingly shrouded all the inner workings of the church in secrecy. The pastoral war stemmed from the associate refusing to keep quiet about the congregation's double life. Instead of allowing the congregation to spin into chaos, the elected leaders could have prepared for their role by learning their governing responsibilities, articulating the guiding vision of the church, and holding their pastors accountable to it—and not allowing such systemic toxicity to grow. Then information management decisions would have been much healthier and more transparent.

Congregations, like families, develop certain communication patterns over time. Information in congregations is frequently managed with secrecy, denial, triangulation, gossip, rumor, innuendo, or "skilled incompetence." Skilled incompetence is a highly developed communication style that covers up real problems. One church governing body used this technique for almost a decade to respond to the intense conflict in the congregation; they claimed to keep doing the best they could, which was actually nothing at all. They had developed a habit of skilled incompetence.

Some congregations tend to skirt the truth, not because it would be truly inappropriate to tell it but simply because it would be painful. Some establish certain patterns for responding to conflict, crisis, or disappointment rather than allowing open expression and maintaining the freedom to make choices appropriate to the situation. Leaders in such congregations may have become hampered by fears about the congregation's demise, the difficulty of change, or increasing diversity. Tacit rules or ways of doing things develop about what can and cannot be done or how members or leaders should behave. Possibilities for creative decision making become limited by enmeshment and protection of individuals, secrets, ideas, various groups, or the congregation's good name. A theme of "we're all in this together," intended to build unity, may instead foster groupthink. When leaders know and address the congregation's historical communication patterns, the decisions they make are much more sound.

A Leadership Myth

Fearing that no one will volunteer if the expectations are too high, congregations downplay the role of leader during recruitment and retain leaders far beyond their effectiveness in their jobs. Congregations cut corners under a mistaken belief that they won't be able to retain leaders if they expect too much of them. This myth of leadership ensures ignorance in areas of information management. In fact, the opposite proves to be true. Recruiting leaders is actually easier when they are given overt expectations, provided with job descriptions and training, and given resources to guide them

through difficult decisions. When the job is made clear and pa-
rameters are set in place, leaders effectively manage even complex
and sensitive information.

Chapter 9

A Decision-Making Process

Every congregation faces decisions about how to manage sensitive information, and some congregations have to make difficult decisions in the midst of crises. Highly stressful situations rarely bring out the best in anyone. Faith leaders can practice making difficult decisions wisely now instead of waiting until a congregational predicament forces them to become instant specialists at information management. Carefully made decisions enhance the congregation's long-term health, without unnecessarily harming individuals. Knee-jerk reactions, especially during a crisis, have lasting negative repercussions. Taking time to seriously pay attention to the *process* of making decisions results in information management that creates a stronger faith community.

This chapter's four-step process works for making all sorts of decisions. Leaders need to (1) assess the situation, (2) consider the options and determine the plan, (3) act, and then (4) evaluate. However, the management of sensitive material is fraught with complexity and nuances. The previous chapter recommended that leaders prepare for the decision making required of them by knowing their own personal issues, their role and responsibilities, and their congregation. Wiser decisions result from such preparation to manage complicated congregational communications. The more attention leaders pay to *each* step in the decision-making process, the more prudent their decisions. If leaders leap into action too quickly, their ineffective information management will result in unexpected problems down the road. When each step is followed, problems are resolved at the time they arise.

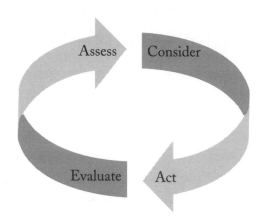

FIGURE 9.1
A DECISION-MAKING PROCESS

Making decisions about information management involves moving through the cycle (assess, consider, act, evaluate). Sometimes the content and amount of the information requires moving through the cycle a number of times. How well leaders have prepared for their task of decision making also affects the efficiency of the process. If the information is sensitive or potentially volatile, communication can be complicated and involve a series of choices to be made. One small change in circumstances can affect the overall situation and the decision-making process will need to be repeated from the beginning. Leaders may need to assess the situation, consider the options, take action, and evaluate the decision in repeated cycles.

Missteps in managing sensitive information tend to compound themselves. One poor decision triggers another and another if each decision isn't evaluated and the next action considered carefully. The decisions Rev. Mackay had to make when a church member confessed that he abused a niece illustrate an all too common challenge in congregations across the country. Clergy regularly gain information that their seminary education did not prepare them to manage—be it about an embezzlement, the secret gambling addiction of a key lay leader, or an illicit romantic relationship between the married choir director and married soloist. Because stories related to child abuse in faith communities have frequented the news, Rev. Mackay's story was selected as a case study to explain the decision-making process and demonstrate how each decision affects the subsequent ones, with helpful or harmful results.

Rev. Mackay's Dilemmas

Lincoln Presbyterian Church, the focal point of a small town of Lincoln, stands within a block of the elementary school and city hall. As in many small communities, everyone in Lincoln seems to know each other—and much private material about others. The community grapevine is as rich a source for information as the local newspaper. Whether members of Lincoln Presbyterian or not, townspeople tend to keep up with the church news. The church's pastor, Rev. Mackay, has joked with a touch of bitterness that if he sneezes, the whole town worries that he has a cold.

In his office one afternoon, Rev. Mackay heard the confession of John Jones, a longtime and beloved member of the church. John told his pastor that he had recently pled guilty to charges of molesting his 12-year-old niece. Concerned for children in the church who might be at risk, Rev. Mackay asked John to worship only at the later service, when fewer children attend, and to come on time and leave immediately after services. John agreed and also promised to let the pastor know any other times he came on the church grounds. Rev. Mackay closed the meeting with prayer and promised John his spiritual support as the court proceedings progressed.

What should Rev. Mackay do with this information about John? When John first left the office, Rev. Mackay was stunned and really had no idea what to do—so doing nothing seemed the best choice. Initially Rev. Mackay decided to "seal" the fact that John had come to see him and the content of the discussion. Rev. Mackay knew that Lincoln church members simply assumed he would take care of things, in particular any issues that were uncomfortable. The prior pastor had handled everything in his 25 years of ministry at the church. Besides, he thought, this church had been traumatized when a member abused a child in the past. As a natural consequence of the prior abuse, many in the congregation were vigilant about perceived threats to children and especially protective of children. He considered keeping quiet to avoid stirring up a hornets' nest.

But after a sleepless night, Rev. Mackay decided he didn't want to be the only leader of the church to know, even if he did think the information really should be kept confidential—so he confided in the highest ranking lay person, Allison, who was Clerk of Session. Telling Allison eased his own stress and loneliness about keeping this information and gave him another person with whom to talk. Presuming no other children were at risk, he and Allison rationalized that no one else should be told. However, they did not realize that their silence might collude with the secret keeping that often protects offenders and damages congregational trust.

Within the week, the situation had shifted. Rev. Mackay discovered that John had told several of his friends in the congregation about the pending court date to garner their support and agreement to appear as character witnesses. Rev. Mackay started receiving angry calls from parents in the congregation about his not warning them that "John is a pedophile." Local citizens called, furious that he never told the nearby elementary school principal. The elders threatened to fire him for irresponsibility and keeping secrets from them. Church staff members were horrified that they were not given the information, especially because they had seen John on the church grounds often and knew nothing of the restrictions on his being there.

Rev. Mackay would have benefited from being better prepared for decision making (becoming a leader in the know) and then using the four step decision-making process, which would have guided him to carefully consider the ramifications of his choices.

Knowing Himself and His Congregation

Faith leaders may explain their decisions with great ethical argument; however, the strongest influence on a decision is often the personal struggles or history of each individual. Rev. Mackay felt overworked and underpaid, while facing a seemingly endless stream of congregational minicrises. When was he supposed to take time to enhance his self-awareness, to know himself and his motivations, much less understand his role in the church? He had not taken the time to explore his own leadership and the personal issues in his life that could affect his ministry. Wasn't he supposed to be all things to all people? He rarely had time for exercise, playfulness, or enjoying the camaraderie of those in his Rotary Club, much less the precious companionship of his wife. He felt a sense of failure and inability to flourish in ministry, which only magnified the voice of his mom in his head. Her chatter haunted him with incessant complaints about his not measuring up to her expectations. Having grown up with much conflict in his family of origin, he usually avoided confrontation and conflict; it was easier to give in or just hope that a problem would simply go away with time. Instead of nurturing his spiritual grounding and increasing clarity about his inner self, Rev. Mackay told himself that "one day" he would take better care of himself, "one day" he would check in with a counselor, and "one day" he would improve his spiritual practices beyond preparation for the sermon each week. Of course, that meant that "one day" his ability to discern more clearly might improve—but not today, he had too much to do. He was hardly prepared to take on one more church decision.

As much as Rev. Mackay wanted to believe that his knowledge about John was his alone to deal with, a pastor makes decisions in the context of a congregation with its own dynamics. Prudent decision making requires a leader to know the congregation well enough to anticipate the effects of various choices. The prestigious Lincoln Presbyterian Church had a troubled history of secrets about the shortcomings of both ordained and elected leaders, including their affairs and addictions. Information was hidden to maintain the church's reputation as an upstanding, solid rock in the community. Over time, those who knew the real story behind the church's public image gained power, and those who were out of the gossip loop became less active or left the congregation.

Rev. Mackay had to make information management decisions in the midst of congregational dynamics that promoted pushing difficult interpersonal matters under the virtual rug. He could unwittingly follow the church's tradition of silencing information that others might need to know, information that may be difficult at first to process but whose transparency is crucial for the health of the congregation. Without examining the context within which he was making decisions, Rev. Mackay was doomed to repeat patterns with which the congregation was comfortable instead of making the most effective, well-discerned choices.

The most crucial question for Rev. Mackay and the congregation should have been about how to ensure the safety of children, but this church had a history of looking the other way when things were haywire. In this congregation, anyone could get away with sexual boundary crossings because they were all trained to ignore what they saw. Like many congregations, Rev. Mackay's church had never considered what to do if a registered sex offender wanted to worship there—much less if one of its beloved members abused a child.

Groups bound by "reciprocally altruistic relationships" developed over a long period of time tend to stifle difficult information.[1] People with close friendships in the congregation tend to avoid disclosing anything that could threaten those bonds. According to sociologist Craig T. Palmer, the repression of negative information is more likely in a congregation than a high-powered business. Members of congregations seek to care unselfishly about and for one another, generation after generation. Their religious values create an expectation of authenticity and mutuality. Instead of settling for the short-term gains produced by deceit and secrecy, most churches expect honesty and openness, which enhance individual and community relationships.

Given the history of the Lincoln church, however, Rev. Mackay was making decisions in a congregation where long-term protection of the church's image trumped long-term healthy relationships. Rev. Mackay may not have been sure of what to do with the information he received, but he knew about the congregation's pattern of silences and pretenses. He knew of the tendency for members to hush volatile or sensitive information in the church, thus leaving a communication void that created an anxiety pit filled with rumor and innuendo. He did not fully understand applicable state laws or his own polity as spelled out in the Book of Order, so he presumed that he didn't have any guidelines to follow. The process outlined in this chapter could have assisted him in making a wiser decision about the information he was handling.

Step 1: Assess the Specific Situation

Concerns, frustrations, and fears can be paralyzing when the information that needs to be dealt with is particularly difficult. Emotions, especially anxiety and anger, limit the ability of leaders to accurately assess the situation they are in. Maybe Rev. Mackay should have processed his own resistance to conflict with a consultant before attempting any problem solving. Processing emotions and thoughts prior to focusing on the decision at hand might have cleared out some confusion and anxiety so that he could then think more objectively. He might have taken a brisk walk, slammed tennis balls, or talked to himself in the shower. Had he taken the dilemma to a committee rather than act as an individual, the group also would have needed a brief time to blow off steam before assessing the situation and getting the facts straight. Emotionality can distract leaders from focusing on the facts, and instead they worry about speculations, rumors, or fear.

Calm decision making, rather than reactivity, tends to promote healing and reduce further harm—especially when information is loaded with potential for creating anxiety or damage. When discerning a solution to information management dilemmas, five key assessment steps help keep the situation contained and controlled rather than it escalating and turning destructive.

Assessing a Situation

1. State the situation and/or dilemma as succinctly as possible.
2. Determine who knows what.
3. Identify all relevant facts:

    -   What is the source of the information?
    -   Who "owns" the information?
    -   Who has a right to know the information?
    -   Who has a need to know?
    -   What history and background is pertinent to the situation?
    -   What information is missing?

4. Determine whether anyone is at risk of foreseeable harm.
5. Investigate applicable rights and rules (policies, laws, and so forth).

---

1. State the Situation as Succinctly as Possible

Personal motivations affect decision making from the very beginning. Rev. Mackay selectively classified as fact the information
with which he was comfortable and ignored relevant information
that was distasteful. Personal interpretations aside, the bottom line
in this case was: John pled guilty to a criminal complaint against
him for molesting his niece, and Rev. Mackay needed to decide
what to do with this information. The clarity of this bottom line
was distorted by Rev. Mackay's worries about how this story could
affect the church's and his success or reputation. As objectively as
possible, reducing the situation to its relevant components reduces
anxiety and distractions from the basic decision at hand.

2. Determine Who Knows What

Before Rev. Mackay decided who else, if anyone, needed to know
the information he had just learned, he should have determined
who else knew it already. When he assumed that only he and John
knew the information, he mistakenly classified the information as
confidential. However, a criminal charge is a public record, a child
abuse charge may appear in the newspaper or on the Internet, and
certainly the story will spread through the town's grapevine. Rev.
Mackay was not the only person who knew about the abuse. Others already knew, but Rev. Mackay treated the information as if it
were confidential, rather than limited access.

    Rev. Mackay could have determined the current level of knowl-
edge simply by asking John a few questions during their initial
meeting. Had John told others in the congregation or friends
outside the church? Who might the niece have told? Because a
criminal charge is public record, Rev. Mackay could have called
the district attorney and verified the information John had given,
without reference to why he was asking. As much as possible, congregational leaders should find out who else knows the information

they are debating about protecting or releasing, no matter what its topic.

3. Identify All Relevant Facts

Answering several key questions helps leaders assess the facts related to a situation and keeps leaders from becoming distracted by less important issues or ones that have no actual connection to the dilemma at hand.

First, leaders should answer the question, *what is the source of the information?* How trustworthy is that source? Under what circumstances was the information received? Rev. Mackay thought he had no reason to distrust the information John gave him, although most people give self-incriminating information a favorable spin to make themselves look better. For this particular story, the county district attorney's office or police department would be a much more trustworthy source than John. Abusers of children and adults easily manipulate clergy into siding with them, portraying themselves as victims and minimizing the seriousness of their abusive behavior.

Another key question for Rev. Mackay and the lay leader he consulted is, *who owns the information?* Whose story was John telling? His own, of course, but also that of his niece. Many stories are dually or even multiply owned. When a wife complains about the messy habits of her husband, the information is also his. When a parent talks about a child's behavior, the story is also the child's. If the information is personal to one person, that individual should control further disclosure. However, a public prayer mentioning John wouldn't be wise, even with his permission, because such a prayer relates to information belonging to his family, the niece, and her family. Multiple ownership complicates who can share the information.

In this situation, Rev. Mackay needed to consider more specifically what *part* of the information was owned by *whom*. To protect confidences, Rev. Mackay could not reveal to anyone other than child protective services that John came to see him or any details about what John told him. Yet after checking with the district attorney to confirm what aspects of the story were public record, he could tell others any information "owned" by law enforcement and the public without mentioning his meeting with John.

A faith leader must also consider the question, *who has a right to know the information?* The state has determined that anyone has a right to know when someone is accused of violating the law; therefore a criminal charge is public information. In fact, if John were already convicted of a sex offense, the public might have access to more information, such as his photograph and residence through the National Sex Offender Registry, www.nsopr.gov. But Rev. Mackay had not considered this general right to know.

Because Presbyterian polity gives authority for governance to the ruling elders on the session (the congregation's board), they had a right to know information necessary to lead the congregation. Therefore, the session had a right to know what Rev. Mackay knew about John because that information was needed to keep the church solvent and safe for worshipers. By not telling the church's ruling elders the public record of John's charges and confession, Rev. Mackay and Allison created greater potential for adverse decisions by those leaders and possibly a lawsuit for failure to protect. John might be asked to chaperone the youth group on a mission trip or made the Sunday school teacher in his niece's class. If the leaders recruiting volunteers did not know the situation, they inadvertently could have put John's niece and other children and youth at risk.

Faith leaders also should consider *who has a need to know the information.* Just because the child abuse charge against John is public record does not mean that everyone has a need to know the information. Rev. Mackay faced a dilemma about whom he needed to inform: the principal of the school across the street or the city library next door? Probably not those two, Rev. Mackay reasoned; law enforcement should be responsible for that, not the offender's pastor. What about the church school director and nursery school teachers? Parents in the church? His initial decision not to tell them drew the harshest criticism, because they considered the children's safety more important than protecting John's reputation and felt they should have been told.

Another question for faith leaders to answer is *what background information is pertinent to this situation*. Personal relationships between a clergyperson and congregant can interfere with wise decision making about whether to reveal or conceal certain information. The fact that John and his pastor regularly played golf meant that their friendship likely clouded Rev. Mackay's ability to make objective decisions. The information about John's offense should have been treated the same as that of a less familiar parishioner confessing the same story. Even if John donated more money to Lincoln Presbyterian than anyone else, the information about his offense should have been treated the same as a less generous donor. John and Rev. Mackay's relationship history, the size of John's pledge, and even John's leadership position in the church were no excuse for bad information management.

Crucial background Rev. Mackay should have considered was the niece's relationship to peers and others in the church. She didn't live miles away; in fact, she was in the church youth group. Some victims of abuse don't talk to anyone about what happened because of their shame. Some teenage girls, however, share very personal information with best friends, and not knowing how to handle such frightening stories, those friends may tell other peers. If John's niece told one or two members of the group, would they also be spreading the story and in need of pastoral care? Discussions with the youth group could give the teenagers tools with which to understand the charges, the dynamics of abuse, and John's niece's pain and anger. When Rev. Mackay didn't check out the niece's relationship to the church, he overlooked a vital factor in the situation.

Last in the string of questions leaders must ask themselves is *what information is missing*. In making his decision only to tell Allison and no one else, Rev. Mackay had not fully determined or measured the risk. He didn't need to know any of the sexual specifics about John's offense; but he did need to know any information that might directly affect members of his congregation or the church itself. If the offense happened on the church property or during a church-sponsored event, the insurance company should have been called immediately. As a pastor, he might want to know if John's family was aware of the story and how it was handling this tragedy. A faith leader need not play detective but does need to recognize what crucial information is missing and find out the facts he or she can, rather than make decisions based on assumptions. Assumptions only create more problems. Wise leaders establish what is factual, discern what else needs to be known, and decide when to back off rather than pry for unnecessary detail.

4. Determine the Risk of Foreseeable Harm

As difficult as certain information may be, the receiver needs to pursue questions of safety. When hearing information that is unpleasant, we often deny or minimize the potential impact—or overreact. If John had embezzled from his employer, what would be the risk to the church? What would need to be disclosed so that they didn't elect him treasurer? If John had a drinking problem, how would that affect the church or its members? Could this information be disclosed if a committee wanted him to drive or chaperone on youth group trips? Regardless of the content of sensitive information, faith leaders need to weigh the potential harm to the individual(s) involved and to the congregation itself. Two questions can help leaders assess risk: (1) Does the information involve child abuse, domestic violence, elder abuse, potential suicide, or other harm? and (2) Whose well-being has been or might be affected?

Few faith leaders have the education or resources to deal with situations as potentially dangerous as interpersonal violence. When personal safety may be jeopardized, leaders are ill-advised to rely on their own resources. Leaders need to tap the expertise of social service providers, consultants, law enforcement, and abuse prevention advocates. Most states have laws that require notifying civil authorities who can give advice or intervene. National Web sites and hotline numbers make it relatively easy for clergy and victims to reach specialized prevention services in their area. Professionals at community agencies can help protect the person at risk, as well as help determine what information should be shared with whom. Effective leaders already have pertinent online resources bookmarked and key phone numbers readily accessible.

John confessed to child abuse, so clearly at least one person had already been harmed. Because civil authorities were already involved, Rev. Mackay may not have needed to report his reasonable suspicions of abuse to child protective services or the police. But what if John was bluffing about the authorities knowing already? As mentioned above, to appropriately assess the situation and to meet his legal and ethical obligations, Rev. Mackay should have reported the niece's abuse anyway—if nothing else, to verify that law enforcement knew the niece needed protection and to document that he called about his concern. If the abuse was already known to authorities, no harm is done by his inquiring. In most states, if John had not been truthful about informing the police and Rev. Mackay failed to report the abuse, Rev. Mackay himself could be criminally liable.

To assess the full situation, Rev. Mackay needs to ask himself who else, besides John and his niece, was harmed by John's behavior. John's wife and family, the niece's family, and ultimately the congregation were or would soon be affected by the story. When congregational leaders consider the breadth of certain information's effect, currently and potentially, they can guide decisions about the flow of information, as well as better focus pastoral care.

Too often we think of harm as abuse, but other forms of damage can result when pieces of information are withheld or shared without discernment. Without a parishioner's permission, one minister tenderly mentioned the man's upcoming surgery for a brain tumor in Sunday prayers. Someone attending the service had sold the parishioner his life insurance policy—and cancelled the coverage the next day. Leaders do well to consider potential risk of harm beyond its common association with abuse.

Investigate Applicable Rights and Rules

Both civil laws and denominational guidelines describe *what* and *how* information may be released, as well as to *whom*. Some limit and some demand information release. What state laws regarding child protection apply in this situation? What statutes and religious guidelines define the information clergy can withhold or hold as confidential? Clergy are wise to check the specific guidelines of their governing body, as well as federal, state, and local laws that may relate to the situation.

Step 2: Consider the Options, Determine the Plan

When journalists compose their articles, they include the basics: who, what, when, where, how, and why? When making information management decisions, congregational leaders should consider these same basic questions, though the order of the questions does not matter.

Determining an Action Plan

1. *Why* conceal or reveal the information?
2. *Who* is the most appropriate person to disclose the information?
3. *To whom* should the information be disclosed?
4. *What* details or information will be shared or withheld?
5. *When* should the information be released?
6. *How and where* is the information disclosed?

---

1. Why Conceal or Reveal the Information?

Why questions unfortunately encourage rationalizations, especially when leaders want to explain away a decision they have already made. Asking why should precede decision making in order to establish the core values, priorities, and purpose. *Why would someone share information* about abuse? To protect other children. Why would someone share information related to a serious conflict? To resolve the crisis. Honestly answering the why question helps leaders acknowledge their motivations. *Why wouldn't information be shared?* It might not be shared to avoid embarrassing the congregation, and when this is spoken aloud, leaders examine their core values more deeply and move toward fuller disclosure.

Rev. Mackay and Allison would have had clear reasons for disclosing what they knew about John's arrest. A prudent disclosure would

- reduce the possibility of more children being harmed
- maintain an atmosphere of transparency in the congregation and minimize anxiety by managing rather than withholding difficult information
- minimize rumors, gossip, and other out of bounds communication
- enhance the trust level within the congregation while encouraging John's accountability and recovery

These are priorities for congregational health, regardless of the content of the information at issue.

2. Who Should Release the Information?

Another way to consider this question is to ask from whom the receiver would most appreciate getting the information. Members of John's congregation may learn about his arrest and court hearings in the local newspaper. Is the journalist the best person to inform them? Is John, Rev. Mackay, a member of the youth group, or a police officer the best person to share the information? Is the grapevine the best way for members of the congregation to hear about the abuse charges related to one of their own? The information was already beyond confidential, even beyond limited access, and openly spreading informally. Were all these talkers the most appropriate people in the congregation to release the information?

If Rev. Mackay had used this four-step process, he would have recognized that he should tell the session the information he had obtained from the district attorney and he needed to tell the church staff. From that point on, the elders on the session could determine who else needed to know about the situation and how to prudently disclose the information.

3. To Whom Should the Information Be Released?

Had Rev. Mackay thought through this question, he could have listed an array of people who should know the correct information about the charges. He should have immediately told the staff who are responsible for children and should have had Allison call a special meeting of the session to tell the elders. As a pastoral gesture, he could have first had a conversation with John to explain his approach. But even if John objected, Rev. Mackay should have gone ahead and told the elders on the session and others directly responsible for children, because they needed to know the already public information and needed to hear it straight from him. Next, the session could have designed a disclosure plan to tell the volunteer teachers and youth leaders, then parents, and finally the whole congregation.

In some cases when no one is in danger of being harmed, an entire congregation would not need to know about criminal charges against a member. When broad dissemination is deemed appropriate, the disclosure may be postponed until the court rules the offender guilty.

At Lincoln Presbyterian, the rumors and gossip already flourished so profusely that telling the whole congregation seemed necessary to correct misinformation with official information.

When sensitive information involves a criminal offense, law enforcement can assist in a decision process about notification of congregational members and others. In some child abuse cases, police detectives have recommended telling all parents with children relatively the same age as the victim(s), because other children may be at risk or have been already been hurt and need help. Rather than make assumptions, Rev. Mackay also could have checked with the police to determine if the library director and school principal had been told about John's arrest. If it were important for them to know, the police would have notified them—and then if anyone angrily called Rev. Mackay, he could respond calmly about the police department's decision to tell or not to tell the church's neighbors. When information is already somewhat available and probably spreading, congregational leaders are wise to determine *all* relevant groups and individuals and include them in the disclosure plan.

4. What Will Be Shared or Withheld?

Rev. Mackay could have confined the information he shared with the session to what seemed necessary and no more. In this situation, police released information such as the alleged offender's name, the charges, and the court date. Guided by what civil authorities considered public, Rev. Mackay could have released that same information to his governing board. The identity of any victim should be protected, of course. Details about the abuse would be unnecessary, distracting, and potentially more anxiety producing.

The church leaders also needed to know about Rev. Mackay's agreement with John, but it had been discussed in the confines of his office and therefore was confidential. So Rev. Mackay could hold another meeting with John, this time with pertinent staff and elected leaders to transform the original restrictions Rev. Mackay had placed on John. A new written covenant could spell out limitations on John's activities related to the church, what the church would offer in the way of pastoral care, and what the ongoing information disclosure plan was. If an offender is truly eager for healing and reconciliation, he or she will agree with and sign such a covenant, understanding that discerned and controlled release of the information is much better than escalating rumor, gossip, and anxiety.

What if John's crime had been embezzlement or sexual harassment of congregational members, or any other problem that could affect the larger body of believers? To protect the well-being of the individual and the congregation, leaders could still design a covenant of appropriate boundaries and plans for revealing or protecting the sensitive information—but only if the clergyperson had not kept such information secret. The integrity and health of a congregation depends on respectful disclosure of information that lay leaders need to know to effectively govern the congregation.

If the sensitive information does not involve criminal behavior, determining what to reveal and what to conceal may be more cloudy. If the rector is divorcing, how much detail is disclosed to the congregation? If the rabbi is in drug rehab, how much information is shared with the leadership or the congregation? If the pastor raids the building fund to cover an unapproved expense, how much is told to others responsible for congregational finances? Generally, leaders should disclose as much information and detail as necessary to carry out effective problem solving and to enhance transparency in the congregation. As people of faith, we often want to explain why bad things happen to good people or why good people make mistakes, so we easily slip into commentary about what might have contributed to certain behavior or what might be true. Yet prudently disclosing sensitive information requires sticking to the facts and the directly related, necessary details without speculation.

5. When Should the Information Be Released?

The sooner leaders assess a situation, plan a response, and implement the plan, the better. Rev. Mackay's hesitation to disclose the

story gave hysteria and anger time to boil around him. Rumors
and gossip filled the information void with erroneous and anxious
babble. If stalled by confusion, Rev. Mackay could have called a
consultant who specialized in these sensitive areas for advice, or
his regional denominational leader, or even the police. He probably
knew he was beyond his usual comfort zone and lacked knowledge
in this area. But instead of reaching out immediately for guidance,
he did what many of us are tempted to do—duck and cover!

Actually Rev. Mackay first dumped John's story on Allison and
then went silent. His impulsiveness had short-circuited his thinking and prevented him from developing a more holistic vision and
taking appropriate action. He told a colleague later he just wanted
John out of his hands and admitted to wanting to cover himself,
so that if anything weird happened he "wouldn't be the only one
holding the bag." Faith leaders need to balance their drive to move
on and get going with the wisdom of prudence and a comprehensive
exploration of options.

The content of information usually affects the timing of its release. The congregation's anniversary dinner is hardly the best time
for disclosing a serious budget deficit that will require dismissing
beloved staff. When leaders struggle to encourage transparency as
well as appropriate confidentiality within their congregations, their
discernment must include right timing—not reacting too fast or
moving too slowly. Rev. Mackay eventually recognized he should
have disclosed the facts to his lay leaders as soon as possible to prevent
further escalation of anxiety and anger in the congregation.

6. How and Where Is the Information Disclosed?

Once a decision has been made to disclose certain information,
leaders remain faced with the decision about the best disclosure
method. Leaders have many ways to share information with their
congregations: individual in-person or telephone conversations,
e-mail, conference calls, letters, worship bulletins, newsletters,
congregational or committee meetings, and so on. Which method

is best depends on the content of the information, as well as who already knows it and the anticipated reaction of those who receive the information.

Of the many options for disclosing information to congregations, e-mail, newsletters, and worship bulletins work well for general announcements but are rarely appropriate when sharing sensitive or potentially volatile information. Conference calls allow more leaders to join a discussion but limit participants' ability to read one another's body language. One-on-one conversations held either face-to-face or over the telephone can be effective if each recipient receives exactly the same information, which requires a script. To be sure that every congregant gets the same information at approximately the same time, a letter to the congregation may precede a verbal announcement and discussion at a large meeting. A letter to the congregation also gives individuals private time to process the contents of the letter.

Recently members at one church received a letter announcing their pastor had been called to another location. Receiving a letter allowed church members to process the information in the privacy of their homes before discussing it in a larger gathering. One church officer quipped, "Thank goodness it wasn't announced in worship." At home, some recipients sobbed and others whooped with delight—awkward responses if in public, when trying to sustain a sense of community. At another church the council wanted to make sure its members opened the crucial letter they would be receiving about the dismissal of their minister for misconduct. So each council member called a specified number of members and read a carefully worded script, not mentioning the misconduct. If anyone on the phone asked for more details, the council member would respond, "For more details, it would be best for you to carefully read the letter you'll receive and to attend the upcoming meeting."

Many questions must be addressed before sending a letter to congregational members. Do they have a *right* or *need* to know the information? Does the mailing list include only members or also

visitors and friends? When such letters disclose sensitive information, its continued spread to the community can be expected.
Wording needs to be precise, the amount of detail carefully considered, the purpose and motivation free of ill intent and hidden
agendas, and transparency balanced with appropriate privacy. All
communication about a situation involving an offence still being
adjudicated needs to clearly say that "the person is charged with"
or "it is alleged that," rather than presuming that she or he has
committed an offense or a crime.

Rev. Mackay could have encouraged the session to send a
brief, carefully worded letter to all church members. The suggested
content could have included the precise wording of the district
attorney's record and a short paragraph from John in which he
admitted that the charges against him were indeed accurate and
publicly apologized for the grief he had caused. The letter could ask
for prayers for John, his family, his niece, her family, and all those
wounded by abuse in their lives. Church members could be invited
to an after-worship gathering led by an outside facilitator during
which they could ask questions, express any concerns, and hear
more about child abuse protection efforts in the congregation.

Faith leaders sometimes rationalize that worship services are
the best time and place to disclose sensitive information with the
general membership. After all, the largest number of people gather
there. But imagine hoping to feel spiritually moved at worship and
instead hearing that the beloved pastor is getting divorced? During
pastoral prayers, one pastor asked for prayers for himself because
he had been asked to resign and didn't know how he would survive
financially. The congregation sat dumbfounded. Whether difficult
information appears in the bulletin, is wrapped in a pastoral prayer,
or is announced during "Joys and Concerns," the resulting anxiety
and pain can derail the focus on worship.

Sometimes disclosure is made best face-to-face. When a rabbi
planned to reveal his sexual orientation to his congregation, he
chose to disclose first in one-on-one, face-to-face meetings with

several congregants whom he anticipated would find the information most difficult. Each was asked not to share the information until the congregational meeting later that week. Because those members had a chance to ask more personal questions in a more private setting and had longer to consider the implications of the information they received, the larger gathering of congregational members was less contentious.

Disclosure can be healing and empowering, but only if leaders carefully think through their plan of action. No perfect option exists; each possibility has drawbacks. Careful consideration is required at every step as leaders determine *why* they should release or conceal certain information, *what* details should be told *by whom* and *to whom*, and *when*, *how*, and *where* the information will be shared. Leaders who have painstakingly and accurately assessed the situation before them and have planned well are ready to move to the next step: action.

Step 3: Act

"Just do it" doesn't work so well when handling sensitive information. Implementing a quick decision may relieve initial anxiety but create more dilemmas in the future. One priest said, "Taking action is easy. It's choosing the right action that is so hard." The discernment done prior to this step makes implementation easier and assures better outcomes.

What if instead of remaining silent, Allison had called a special meeting of the church's elected leaders along with Rev. Mackay? At the meeting, the pastor could have told the lay leaders what had transpired with John. They might have raised their voices, pointed their fingers, and huffed with frustration. At first Allison and Rev. Mackay might wonder if they had made a mistake by including the other leaders. However, after emotions calmed down enough for more reasoned conversation, the lay leaders could then begin their own process of assessing the situation, considering options, and deciding a course of action about how to disclose the information sequentially to the church staff, parents, and whole congregation.

Step 4: Evaluate

Had Rev. Mackay followed this process, he would surely have acknowledged that his decision to initially remain silent and then to tell only the presiding lay leader had had serious repercussions. He, like many of us, had been tempted to resolve an immediate problem expediently, without attention to broader patterns or cumulative effects. Though he had thought silence would prevent anxiety and conflict, silence precipitated just that. Over the years Lincoln Presbyterian had repeatedly suffered from its leaders' mismanagement of sensitive information and secret keeping. Rev. Mackay continued that pattern to the detriment of the congregation and his own ministry. Instead of enhancing the congregation's health, his action contributed to poor communication, a lack of trust, and an increase in rumors and gossiping.

Almost any decision faith leaders make about managing sensitive information will upset someone. If the material is something that congregants would rather not acknowledge, there is no way to release it without causing discomfort and resistance. The information will not be complete enough for someone, will not be released soon enough for another, or by another will be considered inappropriate to even discuss. By carefully evaluating each stage of the process of disclosure, from the content of the letter to the meeting with the parishioners, leaders will maximize trust and build congregational confidence in them to lead and to heal the congregation even in times of great stress. Leaders should listen for constructive feedback and resist being discouraged by unproductive complaints couched as "evaluation."

Anxiety, fear, or confusion on the leaders' part can be contagious. Most congregants are calmed by clear, nondefensive explanations about the various options that were considered and the reasoning behind the decisions their leaders made with due diligence and prayer. The wisest evaluation criterion is not whether others *liked* the decision made, but whether it was indeed made carefully, in consideration of all people involved and the whole congregation, and resulted in minimizing harm and maximizing good. As one leader explained, "Our solution may not have been right, but at least it was authentic; it was based on truth and trust."

Recycling

Often no single action ends the disclosure process. When managing sensitive information, faith leaders usually cycle through the decision-making process many times because a situation often shifts day by day—whether the issue involves a leader's failings, harassment, congregational conflict, financial problems, embezzlement, or another crime within the congregation. Most sensitive information must be handled incrementally due to the layers of discovery and disclosure, especially when revealing longtime secrets. One piece of information triggers questions and the unveiling of yet another piece, or one action shifts the situation that now requires another decision-making process. Potentially volatile issues usually require more recycling through the steps of the process, often during a period of crisis when leaders long for quick and easy answers about what to do. Evaluating each decision made and each action taken increases the probability that the next cycle through the process will be more successful.

Chapter 10

Correcting Poor Communication

W ho reads the mail delivered to the church? Does a church give out addresses or phone numbers of its members? Are minutes of meetings posted or hidden in a file accessible only to the clergy or staff? How is the seemingly mundane information at a congregation dealt with? Does it matter? The whole climate of the church, the spirit of the place and the people, should support healthy practices of information disclosure. The Great Mystery should be God, not a mystery about the location and accuracy of information that is passed around or the way that information will be handled.

Cleaning Up Bad Habits

Of the several negative communication patterns congregations practice, three habits are particularly problematic: triangulation, pass-through communication, and anonymous feedback. While these three may be strategies for getting needs met, they all block rather than help healthy communication. Even if well intentioned, they are deadly habits that in the long run allow people to dodge accountability, gain power, and alienate others. Once everyone understands how to break these habits, those who persist will eventually have to stop or they will become so uncomfortable and isolated that they leave the congregation. To clean up bad communication habits, congregations can do three things: reduce the triangulation, eliminate pass-through communication, and reject anonymous feedback.

Reducing Triangulation

When Betty joined Epworth Church, she wasn't sure how to fit in. She had been a homemaker all of her life, and while she wanted to be involved in the congregation, she wasn't confident about taking on a leadership role. She read an announcement in the bulletin one day that the congregation needed kitchen help for an upcoming potluck dinner. Betty eagerly volunteered. People helped her at the event, but a lot of things about the kitchen were unfamiliar to her. She did her best to put things back where they belonged. A few weeks later she sat by Dorothy at the women's society meeting, and over lunch Dorothy told her in a whisper, "Francine was really upset with the way you left the kitchen." Betty was dumbfounded and silently brooded about this. Not knowing how to resolve the issue, she determined not to volunteer again.

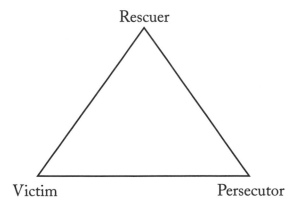

FIGURE 10.1
DRAMA TRIANGLE

These three women were engaging in what is known in counseling theory as triangulation. Francine didn't want to confront Betty directly. To do so would have meant taking responsibility for her feelings, her reactions, and her relationship with Betty. Instead, she enlisted Dorothy and created a relationship triangle. Relationship triangles usually involve three people who each take one of three roles: victim, persecutor and rescuer.[1] Francine placed Betty in the role of persecutor for not putting things back where they belonged. She took on the role of the victim, because she had to clean up after Betty. And then by complaining to Dorothy, she recruited Dorothy to be the rescuer. Dorothy's complicity meant that Betty and Francine could never repair their new relationship. Dorothy may think she is agreeing to a simple communication, but she is really creating more tension and harming the relationship between Betty and her new parish.

While people often suggest that venting is good for the soul, it is actually not very productive. Venting to someone about a third person is simply an avoidance technique. Francine never had to own up to her overly proprietary feeling about the church kitchen. She may have played the victim, but she was also the persecutor. Betty had nowhere to turn to resolve her hurt feelings about the situation. She may have been cast as the persecutor, but she was actually the victim. Once in a triangle, people change places among its three points. The only way to stop the triangulation is for each person to communicate his or her feelings, concerns, or opinions directly to the other.

Dorothy needed to say to Francine, "I don't want to pass your concerns on to Betty. You can share your issues with her or decide that it's not important enough to pursue." She could also send a stronger message to Francine such as, "If you decide not to talk with Betty, then don't keep bringing stuff up; just move on." Dorothy had another strategy that she could use if Francine seemed resistant to talking directly to Betty. If she could stay neutral and uninvolved in the drama, Dorothy could facilitate a conversation between Francine and Betty.

Of course, the best communication strategy is to avoid being recruited into a triangle in the first place. But so often well-intentioned faith leaders and congregants listen to another person's concerns, feelings, or opinions, then realize they inadvertently let themselves be co-opted into involvement, sometimes even taking sides. Once in a triangle, escape may take some courage and clarity but is possible. The triangulated person can redirect the other person straight to the appropriate individual or committee—the one actually involved in the personal issues or the one that can address the concern or mend the relationship. A three-way conversation sometimes helps, but only if the third party facilitates without taking sides or having an agenda, without speaking for one of the other parties, and without adding to the emotional drama.

Eliminating Pass-through Communication

Some congregations get in the habit of pass-through communication. To get a message to someone, you tell someone else. Triangulation is talking about *feelings, opinions, or personal issues* regarding some person or group with the third party, instead of with the person or group actually concerned. Someone angry with the pastor might tell a friend and recruit her to go to the church office to tell the pastor. Pass-through information also involves three parties, but the content of the information is less emotional and personal— sometimes as simple as the expected outcomes of a meeting.

FIGURE 10.2
PASS-THROUGH INFORMATION

With both triangulation and pass-through communication, few people take responsibility for what is accurate and few people speak directly to each other. At bell choir practice each week, two of the ringers passed information back and forth between their husbands about the committees the men were on. The husbands may have been right that it saved them at lot of phone calling to let the women do the talking, but it damaged the working relationship between the two committees because the indirect communication led to confusion and anxiety.

Informal channels of pass-through communication lead to misunderstandings down the road. Like the children's telephone game, the content usually becomes distorted and often the necessary action delayed. In any multiple-staff setting, congregational members make the assumption that whatever they tell one staff person will get to the other(s). When Bill's wife died, he told the church receptionist, fully expecting the information to get to the senior pastor. The church receptionist told the secretary, who passed it to the associate pastor who thought it was just an FYI that didn't need any action on his part. He never passed it to the senior pastor, who didn't learn of the situation until days later, and by that time the family members were both grieving and fuming.

Miscommunication like this may occur unintentionally, but individuals or groups also can use pass-through communication to divide congregations and stir up conflict. A church secretary, unhappy with a new clergy couple in the role of pastor and associate pastor, began using pass-through communication. The secretary avoided direct communication with the female senior pastor Kate, who was her supervisor. Instead, she repeatedly asked Kate's husband, the associate pastor, to pass information to his wife. This indirect communication created more and more distance between Kate and the secretary, and their lack of cooperation began to affect others. The more they didn't talk to each other, the more they talked about it to others. The secretary didn't consciously intend harm; in fact she thought she would solve her personality problems with Kate in this way. But her communication end-run eroded the possibility of resolving her issues with Kate and resulted in more lasting damage.

Giving the message to whomever is close by and expecting him or her to pass it on may seem expedient. When a congregation has copastors, pass-through communication can be particularly problematic. There is no substitute for the direct message. And like triangulation, pass-through communication must be stopped for healthy congregational functioning. Again, the individual being asked to pass something on has the power to stop the pattern. A simple statement such as "I'm not comfortable carrying that message" or "I might mix up what you've said, so perhaps you could call him yourself" is very helpful. The intended messenger needs to clarify why that person is talking to him or her instead of the individual who needs the information. If he or she is dodging responsibility for direct communication, the intended messenger should be all the more determined to stop the pass-through effort.

Rejecting Anonymous Feedback

Ron had a solid tenure behind him as rabbi of the Shalom Center on the campus of a Midwest university. Then some of his board members became angry about political views he expressed in a sermon one week. One of them began sending a series of letters, unsigned, to other leaders and directly to Ron in an effort to have him removed. Each recipient read the letters and began to be affected by them. While some board members suspected who was writing the letters, the uncertainty of the sender's identity limited the ability of the board members to address his or her concerns; so they decided the letters should be ignored. Yet the letter writing continued and became increasingly malicious. Ron became anxious about being personally attacked. He called a meeting and asked that the board find a more active way to respond. But the board focused on guessing who wrote the letters instead of problem solving, and, worse, it appeared that some of the leaders were beginning to believe the totally false accusations in the letters. Finally, Ron acted on his own and posted the letters on the outside of his office door with a note asking the person spreading the inaccurate information to attend the next board meeting to explain his or her concerns directly. No one came to the meeting, but the letters stopped.

Why would someone send letters anonymously? Anonymity allows people to avoid accountability for the content. The individual with the complaint or accusation may also fear reprisals. Sometimes the individual simply doesn't know whom to talk to about a concern. At other times the individual is trying to get his or her way in a conflicted situation, but stays underground to maintain the appearance of being in a harmonious relationship with other congregants. The person sending malicious letters about Ron saw his political statements as an opportunity to fire him, but instead of dealing with the issue through conversations at the board meeting as others had done, he sent anonymous salvos to avoid direct confrontation and responsibility for his own perspectives.

Congregations often ask for anonymous feedback without weighing the potential damage. Evaluations and surveys on clergy effectiveness often open every aspect of the clergy's work and personal life to scrutiny. One unknown congregant criticized a female pastor for not polishing her baby's shoes and having long, instead of short, hair. Such personal attacks are harmful even if they are not anonymous. But when the source of the judgment is unknown, the damage increases because conversation with the source is impossible. The motivation or root concern for such a comment cannot be determined and any real issues cannot be addressed. Was the real critique the pastor's lack of professionalism or were the comments based on the parishioner's discomfort with female clergy in general? There is no way to know when the complainer refuses to be identified.

Instead of generalized, unsigned surveys, congregational ministry evaluations should focus on specific questions regarding the fit between the congregation and the clergyperson or the match between stated vision and actual practice. Members could be asked about various aspects of the congregation's ministry, mutual goals, and the achievement of those goals. The evaluation would give those involved a chance to see if their vision of effective ministry is a shared with others.

Effective evaluations and the ability to adjust congregational goals, activities, and attitudes depend on participants signing their names to their comments. Prior to an evaluation, planning committees can decide who will review the completed surveys and tell the congregation who those people will be and how those comments will be processed. More transparency in the process reduces anxiety and increases the likelihood of participation.

Those who are uncomfortable with the evaluation process can carry their concerns directly to appropriate smaller committees. For example, clergy concerns can be directed to the pastoral relations or mutual ministry committee, concerns about adult classes to the religious education committee, staff issues to the personnel committee, and so forth. While insisting that anonymous feedback will be ignored, congregations should also provide clear and easy channels for members to express their concerns directly.

Also, personnel committees and other groups that oversee pastoral ministry must be clear in their policies and practices that they will neither receive nor take seriously anonymous complaints— letters, phone messages, e-mails, or pass-through communication. Slanderous comments in particular should not be disseminated by the recipient, not even to the clergyperson or any others on a committee, unless the content contains serious threats or requires a legal response. Congregations can waste a lot of energy on slanderous static that interferes with their listening to and addressing real issues. If e-mails are sent from unknown sources, they can be stopped by a trusted leader sending a letter to the congregation asking everyone to block the anonymous sender of the "junk" information and to ignore the content.

When someone refers to anonymous others by saying "and I know that a lot of other people feel that way too," this person is trying to bolster his or her argument. When Pastor Daniel came under attack by a parish family, the family thrived on being known as the individuals leading the assault. But in an effort for family members' complaints to seem more serious and their side to be larger than it actually was, they would say in letters and monologues at meetings that "other people" agreed with them, that "Mr. So-and-so" had been horribly offended by the pastor, and that "many" were withholding their pledge. First, the council invited the "other people," Mr. "So-and-so," and the "many" mentioned to bring their complaints to the council personally and firmly announced that unless those comments were directly brought to the council's attention, they would have to be ignored rather than addressed. The person with the complaint who refers to an anonymous gang of similarly minded folks simply needs to be told, "Your opinion matters to me, and your opinion alone is enough to get my attention. If other people want to bring their opinion, they will need to come to me directly, too."

Anonymous communication is damaging to everyone in the congregation because feelings are often expressed but cannot be resolved. Wounds are named but cannot be healed. Criticism is offered without the chance to explore the possibility of healing. To stop anonymous feedback, clergy and lay leaders need to agree that it is counterproductive. You can't apologize to anonymous. Anonymous will remain angry or sad until he or she comes forward with the truth. Anonymous others cannot and should not be considered when making leadership decisions or resolving conflicts.

A congregation can greatly reduce negative criticism and unresolved hard feelings with these simple and clear boundaries: no triangulation, no pass-through information, and no anonymous communication. When recruited into a communication triangle or to pass information on to another person, leaders need the mantra, "Please tell the person (or committee) directly yourself." When asked to respond to anonymously obtained information, leaders need to simply refuse to consider it substantive until the anonymous person is willing to more clearly own his or her concern. Congregational communication can sometimes hide secrets, agendas, and conflict. As clearer boundaries and transparency in communication may cause negative aspects of congregational life to come into the light, they also reveal the strength, commitment, and love that bind the congregation together—ultimately giving more courage to faith leaders to address any negative dynamics that hinder their faith journey as a community.

How to Clean Up Bad Communication Habits

- Speak directly to the person or committee that the issue concerns.
- Refuse to carry a message from one person or group to another.
- If two people talk with you about each other, offer to meet with both of them together or to find them a mediator.
- If a person complains to you about someone else but refuses to directly talk with the person to resolve the problem, ask him or her to stop talking to you or others about it.
- Reduce venting by first listening and then asking what action the person will undertake to resolve the problem.
- Refuse to take nonspecific or anonymous feedback seriously.

Dealing with Unauthorized Communication

Sometimes in congregations, information spreads around that shouldn't. Information gets leaked that was supposed to stay within a committee, rumors spread when enough information isn't available, and gossip can turn toxic. In leaks, the unauthorized communication exceeds the appropriate or agreed upon boundaries of who should know the information, as when a clergyperson shares a confidential story. In rumors, the communication is inaccurate and therefore not authorized because it is simply wrong, as when representatives of a congregation stormed the bishop's office after erroneously believing that their church might be closed. In gossip, information is shared without its owner's permission or authorization.

Reducing Information Leaks

In her terse manner, social sage Ann Landers often warns, "No secret is secure when it goes beyond the boundaries of two people. This is one statement you can take to the bank." People have great difficulty holding information without spreading it. Personnel committees deal with employee difficulties and are required to keep those stories between committee members. Governing councils struggle with issues that should be contained until an appropriate, planned time to share them with the congregation. A committee chair might say, "The information needs to be limited to our committee until we have better resolution of the issue." But when members of leadership bodies hold extremely uncomfortable information, they may process their pain or confusion with spouses or friends, who are then asked to keep silent. Those spouses and friends are left holding information that is extremely uncomfortable (or titillating) for them, and they process it with others who are then asked to keep silent. But the information keeps trickling out.

Unauthorized communication in the form of leaks occurs when formal, agreed-upon boundaries for certain information are not honored. The causes of leaks vary. Many faith leaders innocently assume that just telling so-and-so does not make much difference, because so-and-so knows how important it is not to repeat the information—but then repeats it anyway. Some leaders simply lack sufficient training about how to manage personal and congregational information. Sometimes a leader leaks information because his or her personal interest supersedes that of the congregation or the individuals involved in the leaked material. For example, after annual staff evaluations, one personnel committee member with a grudge against the administrator could not resist the temptation to repeat uncomplimentary tidbits about her.

Planning can reduce communication leaks. Leaders need to be recruited and elected based on their trustworthiness, not according to popularity or longevity. Leaks are less common among leaders known for their integrity and wisdom.

In addition, committees of the congregation can develop policies that describe how information will be solicited, used, and shared. Which aspects of congregational life will be considered confidential or limited access? Who will know about giving records? What personnel committee issues will be disclosed to other committees in the congregation or the congregation as a whole? What agreements can committees make about limiting access to the information the committee handles? What are the sanctions for members who violate congregational agreements about handling private, confidential, limited-access, and public information?

After leaders have been trained about (1) how to manage sensitive information based on denominational and local congregational policies, (2) legal issues affecting inappropriate disclosure, and (3) the differences among confidential, limited-access, open, and public levels of information, they can be asked to sign a communication agreement to uphold the high standards and pledge accountability for their behavior. Planning to reduce leaks also requires educating the congregation about the communication guidelines leaders have established, so that those guidelines can become standard practices throughout the congregation.

When leaks could do severe damage to the members or staff of a congregation, leaders may be in over their heads and are smart to call in an outside consultant. If the information is volatile, an outside consultant can be especially helpful in processing the information while protecting the congregation against unnecessary litigation, as in a case of sexual abuse. Having a professional outsider listen to leaders' rage, frustration, and other emotions reduces the likelihood of the material being passed on to others. A consultant also can bring objectivity and guide future decisions about information management.

A congregation's communication policy should include holding members accountable for any information they leak. Consequences of not honoring agreed-upon information boundaries might include removing the violator from the committee, requiring that he or she write letters of apology to affected parties, or if boundary violations are repeated and serious, dismissal from the congregation. Patterns of information leakage also suggest a reevaluation of leak reduction strategies.

Other damage control after information leakage depends on the situation. The wife of a pastor who molested a child in the congregation agreed to tell no one else about the situation for four days, so the governing council could meet and all hear about the pastor's abusive behavior at the same time. When she broke her promise and told some friends on the council, the repercussions for the council, congregation, and denomination were explosive. Once the word was out, it couldn't be "put back in the bottle." The unauthorized disclosure triggered rampant gossip and even newspaper articles. The rapidly escalating drama couldn't be slowed. Leaders of the congregation, special crisis management consultants, and denominational officials spent hours unraveling the tangle of emotions, allegations, and disciplinary procedures for the pastor. After the initial trauma calmed for the church and the families involved, the leaders evaluated what patterns within the congregation contributed to the pastor's wife not honoring the agreement to limit access to the information for four days. What they discovered were decades of poor information management, layers of secrets, and no accountability for leaks, rumors, or gossip. Had the congregation been a place of integrity and trust, such a leak might not have happened. Of course, had the congregation been a transparent community, the abuse might not have happened either!

Congregations can reduce information leaks by

- electing to leadership trustworthy people who have shown their integrity and wisdom
- developing formal communication policies setting clear boundaries for information sharing and sanctions for those who don't maintain those boundaries
- asking leaders to sign covenants or agreements to honor the communication boundaries
- educating the entire congregation about the covenant, how to manage information without secrecy, and the responsibility of parishioners to help their leaders abide by the agreement
- inviting an outside therapist or consultant to help leaders process information that may be especially difficult to protect

---

Dispelling Rumors

Congregations too often do business in the parking lot and information flies through the telephone lines. Leaks are one form of unauthorized communication that occurs when information is released in spite of agreements to protect it. As explained in chapter 3, rumors are another form of unauthorized communication, but they are actually misinformation produced in the absence of accurate information. Because a history of distrust and suspicion in the congregation fosters these forms of communication, the best prevention for unauthorized information is creating an open, authentic community. Rumors spread more easily and are more dangerous in *pseudogemeinschaft*—literally an assumed partnership or false sense of community.

Members of a secular service club share an interest or common goal, but the club isn't usually referred to as a community. Being in community suggests something deeper, that members are more interconnected emotionally—like a faith community. Some congregations profess their supportive interconnection but instead are more like *pseudogemeinschaft*, having the appearance of community but not the spirit of true partnership. Sometimes the common interest for congregational communities is not actually living the faith but protecting their historical building, practicing certain rituals, or simply maintaining a connection, healthy or not, that members have grown used to.

Members of a church governing board found themselves experiencing *pseudogemeinschaft* when they discussed how to increase the congregation's membership. The board chair asked, "Why would someone join this church?" What followed was an uncomfortable silence. Finally, one leader suggested people might appreciate the beautiful stone building; another added some people would like the formal worship style. No one mentioned the beliefs that the members of that community held in common or members' unselfish concern for one another. As they continued to talk, they sadly realized that they were really *pseudogemeinschaft* and not the authentic, compassionate community they could be. As a result of its facade, the congregation had suffered from dramatic staff departures and was rife with rumors and secrets about its past. Members' assumed familiarity with one another disguised their lack of crucial information—a void easily filled with rumors. The problems in this congregation did not resolve until its leaders transformed *pseudogemeinschaft* into an authentic and transparent community.

The more authentic a congregation and its leaders become, the more rumors can be addressed quickly and dispelled. After a time of listening, observing, and receiving consultation, the new pastor at Grace Methodist made the decision to open a church secret about the previous pastor (a secret that members knew but were afraid to mention). Shocked parishioners met for a painful but liberating meeting to break open layers of other secrets from the previous ministry. That night they made a commitment to become a transparent congregation in which privacy and confidentiality would be respectfully honored and church business would be "above board from here on out." Over time, the parishioners traded *pseudogemeinschaft* for a community of honesty and love.

In addition to strengthening transparency and community, faith leaders might use other prevention strategies to inhibit rumor mongering. They can

- build a track record of trust and candor against which rumors can be gauged
- make sure needed information is available (in a timely manner) and that formal communication sources are candid and credible
- reduce the systemic anxiety that tends to feed rumors and reduce discernment
- develop "dead-enders" (people who refuse to participate in the grapevine)

Instead of being in denial about the destructive results of rumors and their own complicity with them, clergy and lay leaders first must be role models and name the behavior as negative and unacceptable. As role models, they can each become a "dead-ender"—a person who stops a rumor. A dead-ender may inquire about the rumor's authenticity, asking a question such as, "How do you know that?" A dead-ender may be able to provide accurate information and add, "I don't participate in the spreading of rumors, and I don't want you to do that either." Dead-ending leaders adhere to communication guidelines and then teach others to be dead-enders too. If just a third of the congregation refuses to participate in spreading rumors (or for that matter pass-through communication or triangulation), the whole congregation's patterns of communication will change.

When a rumor passed through coffee hour that the secretary was breaking up with her husband because she had fallen in love with the new associate pastor, a dead-ender came to the rescue.

When the information reached the dead-ender, she told the rumor spreader, "Maisy, it only hurts the congregation for you to suggest there's an affair."

"Well, something is up," Maisy replied.

"Maisy," the dead-ender insisted, "if something is up, we'll know about it eventually and the personnel committee will handle it. For now it's our job to love and support the secretary and the new pastor and to focus on the mission of the church. I want you to stop passing rumors along to me or anyone else."

Some rumors develop and spread slowly and are whispered about with an air of secrecy until nearly everyone has heard them. Other rumors spread quickly because they deal with an immediate threat or concern. Irrelevant rumors tend to dissipate; others require dead-enders providing deliberate intervention. Wildfire rumors especially require prompt and vigorous action on the part of faith leaders. Once opinions start to form based on these rumors, it becomes increasingly difficult to put an end to them. Like prejudices, which harden with time, the more established and rehearsed the opinion, the more resistant it is to counterargument.

Every congregation needs a rumor control center (1) to ensure the members receive complete and accurate information in regular communication, (2) to develop confidence and faith in leaders, which helps the congregation abide its frustrations with protected and limited information at times of suspicion and distrust, (3) to issue as much news as quickly as possible to fill the vacuum of ambiguity with reliable information, and (4) to make reliable information and authoritative interpretation readily accessible, so false tales can be quickly and easily refuted.[2]

Troubled congregations might be helped if they used their governing board as the rumor control center and by paying attention to prevailing rumors and gossip and insisting on accuracy checks. The board could spend a short time at each meeting correcting misinformation heard through the grapevine and channeling concerns, opinions, and other information to the appropriate committee or ministry team. To address a rumor, leaders should expose its existence and provide prompt, unequivocal disproof of the rumor, logically refuting the assertion with counterarguments. To reduce panic and prevent damage, they should quickly disseminate vital, accurate information.

As researchers specializing in rumors, Ralph L. Rosnow and Gary Alan Fine say that in secular settings, derogating or demonizing the person who started or passed the rumor effectively squelches rumors. But when some congregations have used this method, it has only created more shame and underground behavior—and triggered successful defamation lawsuits. Belittling or criticizing somebody in a congregation also violates the religious call to love one another in spite of behavior.

Congregations must find ways to respectfully hold people accountable for negative behavior. Faith leaders might directly confront rumormongers; ask where they got the information they spread, how they decided to spread it, and if they realized the information was incorrect; and tell them to stop spreading inaccurate information. By trying to understand a rumormonger's motivations for passing on the rumor, leaders can try to address the problem fueling the motivation. Some habitual rumor spreaders just need attention, some have lost power they previously had and are still trying to manipulate the congregation, and some may simply enjoy the excitement of creating chaos in the church family system.

Often a rumormonger simply lacks necessary information, hears an explanation he or she needs to reduce anxiety, and assumes the explanation to be factual. With careful attention to affirming the individual while correcting the behavior, some individuals with lousy communication patterns can change their behavior. If not, congregational leaders must isolate habitual rumor spreaders from any positions of real or tacit power and set strict boundaries for their behavior, including consequences for spreading rumors again.

Encouraging *Godsibb* rather than Gossip

Gossip is the third kind of information spread outside formal information channels. Congregants naturally share personal information about one another. The challenge is to reduce harmful gossip and promote respectful, pastoral conversation—to restore gossip to its original meaning and the notion that we are siblings in God. To hold someone in your thoughts, speech, and prayers as a child of God creates fresh opportunities to exercise compassion and to create interconnection. *Godsibb* conversation is honest, direct, free from prejudice or bias, and informative without being invasive. What might have remained unredeemed is now made available for healing, mercy, and change.

To transform standard gossip into "godsibb," information that belongs to another person may be shared with no judgment or advice giving, only with comfort, honesty, and prayerful concern. Theologian William Willimon explains that a "forgiven sin is no longer the subject of continued conversation,"[3] so forgiven shortcomings would not be fodder for "godsibb." If the personal information belongs to someone other than the speaker (as it does in gossip), a true sibling in God would ask the owner of that information for his or her permission before passing the story along. That request would verify the accuracy of the story, as well as honor the person.

Dean didn't mind people in his congregation knowing about his radiation and chemotherapy; what he hated was how the information was transmitted as gossip. People tended to add commentary about how Dean shouldn't have been surprised he ended up with lung cancer after all his years of smoking, about what they thought he should be doing with the last 18 months the doctors predicted he would live, or about how his wife would be better off without him. He had given permission for others to know about the cancer but not for gossip. Dean had hoped for some compassionate "godsibb." The saying "If you don't have anything nice to say, don't say anything" works well for congregations too. Negative commentary, opinions, advice, and judgment about someone else's life are better not shared at all.

Unfortunately most of us are not used to "godsibb." Sometimes giving personal information to a prayer group is not much different from publishing it in the church newsletter; it will get out. Unlike rumors, gossip has some basis in fact, though facts are distorted and exaggerated by the teller and many tellings. Like the rumor control centers mentioned above, congregational leaders and governing councils need to pay attention to prevailing gossip, insist on accuracy checks and permission from the subject of the gossip before the information is shared further (or they must stop the sharing), and conscientiously direct concerns and out-of-bounds information to appropriate or designated channels. If information is misdirected, it should be sent to the proper committee or ministry team.

As you can see, telling the truth is more complicated than ever imagined. Leaders and clergy need to painstakingly consider what to do with the information they gain, maintain, and release in their role as information trustees. They need to name and hold members accountable for communication behaviors that are negative and damaging. They also need to teach and model communication behaviors that enhance the faith community. Congregations need to aim for integrity and transparency, so that their self-image matches the internal reality and they are truly communities of people in supportive relationships.

Chapter 11

Special Circumstances

In Mary's first assignment as a new parish priest, she quickly learned that her predecessor was still an active member of the congregation. How would the congregation's ongoing communications with him affect her authority and ability to lead the congregation? She wondered if he would be given more honor and respect because of his age, gender, and years of experience, and what would happen if he voiced opinions about changes she might make.

When Shane became the board chair of his congregation, he learned that several incidents of sexual misconduct in the church's history had been swept under the rug. What should he to do with that information?

When Rabbi Marc went to his first midsized congregation, he was astonished by the way information was passed from the secretary to others on staff and that anything people shared in a home visit with the previous rabbi was passed along as if it had been splashed on billboards for others to know. This lack of communication boundaries made him extremely uncomfortable, but how could he address this problem?

When a congregation holding a controversial holy union service for a lesbian couple learned that the press had been informed of the date and time of the event, lay leaders weren't sure what to do about the possibility of media frenzy.

In each of these situations what would be ideal is for leaders to have developed a plan, created or reviewed policies, and built up their confidence in handling communication quandries. With each unique circumstance, obtaining as much background information as possible and listening to the concerns and stories of those most directly affected are crucial tasks. Even if leaders must take up the task of loving confrontation, they can act with integrity when they communicate and disclose information appropriately.

Reclaiming the Past

After his first year as senior pastor, Miguel decided to enlist the leaders of Covenant Community Church in putting together a complete history of their faith community. He looked for a way to hear the stories beneath their stories because he was confused by awkward silences during certain discussions, and he had noticed that there were subjects they seemed to avoid. He had an intuitive feeling that they hadn't disclosed pieces of their history and didn't talk about them publicly. So he brought a long roll of butcher paper to a leaders' retreat, rolled it out on the floor across the room, and marked it off in decades. He gave everyone a marking pen and asked the leaders to make a timeline of events in the congregation's life since its inception.

The history-telling process began with the first pioneer pastor and the first building. Miguel encouraged them to dig deeper. "Who were these people, and why did they follow Jesus?" "What motivated them to join this congregation?" As the leaders added more symbols and stories, they began to hesitate. With some nervous laughter, they revealed that a pastor had totally trashed their parsonage. Then they were silent. Finally someone admitted that one pastor had engaged in sexual relationships with teenaged girls in the congregation, back when no reporting laws and helping agencies existed. The congregation had been frozen with fear that this could happen again, and rather than take steps to abuse-proof the congregation, they simply pretended it never happened. "We can't put that in the history brochure in the pew pocket!" one of them said. The others groaned, releasing years of tension that held this secret in place. After the events were recorded on the paper rolled out on the floor, the stories seemed to have less power. Miguel worked with the leaders to tell the congregation's story in a way that transformed their shame into a commitment to ensure all worshipers' safety.

Another minister faced a challenge similar to Miguel's when she discovered the public but secret criminal record of sexual abuse by a popular church member. On a home visit, the man's cousin told the minister the shocking story. The minister then checked the state's sex offender registry and verified the accuracy of the story and the public nature of the church member's offender status. After she centered herself in prayer, she called together the governing body of the congregation. The leaders agreed to send a letter to the church's parents inviting them to a meeting to discuss children's safety, as well as to create a covenant with the child-offending member, both welcoming him and setting boundaries. At that meeting, parents learned personal safety skills to teach their children, as well as heard a brief explanation of the abuse charges against the church member. Instead of escalating fear, the open conversation gave the parents an opportunity to express their concerns, hear what the church was doing to protect children, receive knowledgeable responses to their questions, and learn how to better protect their children without creating paranoia. Opening the secret, which everyone knew but was afraid to discuss, deflated an intense anxiety that had plagued the congregation, and it enhanced the transparency and compassion of their faith community.

Talking about the brokenness of the congregation makes it easier for members to talk about their individual brokenness. When a congregation models a path to wholeness, its members can find personal wholeness as well. The guidelines for open discussions about church history provided on page 208 will give parishioners a place to start in letting others know that this is an ordinary congregation

---

Reclaiming the Past

Use this list of suggestions to elicit increased levels of
disclosure about a congregation's history:

- Use already developed communication guidelines and
  review them at the beginning of the conversation.
- Compile a history of the congregation that includes *all* of
  the history.
- Gather information about the years when information
  gaps appear or rumors abound.
- Invite people to tell about their personal experiences and
  what they observed, without speculation or accusatory
  commentary.
- If any questions surface about the truthfulness of a
  statement, remind people that the claims are alleged
  (as in *alleged* abuse, *alleged* embezzlement, *alleged* sexual
  misconduct).
- Respectfully acknowledge any remaining wounds and
  avoid blame related to any negative situations.
- Establish healing conversations with those who have
  been wounded and those who previously helped to cover
  up information.

---

of real people. Within any congregation are people who have
lived through painful interpersonal conflicts, boundary crossings,
and damaged trust. They have survived threats from the culture
outside the congregation and wounds within it. They have coped
with painful situations and gone through times of reconciliation
and healing. They have, through faith in God, offered forgiveness,
restored trust, and been resilient.

People who acknowledge their brokenness humbly before God
draw others into their walk of faith. The transparent congregation

creates outreach and evangelism through the integrity of its leaders. People are glad to join an organization where people are true to the ideals of their faith and willing to acknowledge when they have fallen short. Revisiting history is often a crucial part of the journey toward becoming a repentant and restored community.

Handling Information about Donors

Clergy, lay leaders, and members of congregations may have different views about handling financial records, especially about who should have access to them and whether clergy or designated laity ought to know what is in those records. Clergy may believe it is up to them to decide what they should know about the trends or details of congregational records, while members in their congregations may believe they have the authority to decide who knows what.

Actually, who knows detailed information about congregational finances is less about the information itself than about the power of holding it. As the old adage goes, "information is power." The more people know, the more power they have in shaping the current and future life of the congregation. When individuals with knowledge of giving records withhold that information from lay leaders designated to govern the congregation, those leaders make decisions without full knowledge of relevant data, and their power and ability to lead the congregation is limited. When clergy don't know the names of donors or levels of donors' gifts to the congregation, they know less than lay leaders about the financial status of the congregation, including the giving potential of the congregation, giving trends, and who is withholding funds in times of congregational conflict. Without knowledge of the donor data and income patterns of the congregation, both lay and ordained leaders are less able to lead effectively.

Of course, full disclosure may also be risky. Both clergy and laity who know the size of an individual's donation may be tempted to misuse the information. Those who know the name of a major

donor may try to honor that person with leadership roles and responsibilities, regardless of his or her leadership competency; they
might be unduly influenced in their decisions and vote in alliance
with a major donor; or they may try to keep a donor happy by
catering to his or her ideas about the mission and ministry of the
congregation. On the other hand, some clergy and laity become
bitter about a member's lack of financial participation in the congregation. When both clergy and a few key lay leaders know this
information, they are able to provide checks and balances for each
other and to hold one another accountable for good boundaries
and the ethical use of information within the congregation.

Clergy opinion about knowing donor data varies. Some clergy
do not want to know specific information at all; some clergy ask to
know only who gives but not how much, or to be informed about
significant changes in giving levels—either up or down. Some pastors closely watch parishioners' giving patterns throughout the year
and from year to year and view that information as a clue about
whether pastoral care is needed. When a family reduces or ends
its donations to the church, some clergy want to know if family
turmoil has challenged the family's financial stability or if a family member was hurt by something that happened at church or is
angry about some aspect of the ministry. What does the change
in giving indicate about family health or satisfaction?

When clergy say, "I don't want to know about the donors,"
their resistance often reflects personal anxiety or maybe an old
taboo against talking about money. They may also be afraid that
the congregation will accuse them of using this information preju-
dicially. Certainly both clergy and lay leaders can do great harm
by disclosing financial information indiscreetly or letting the size
of a donation affect leadership decisions. When clergy and leaders talk openly about their fears and raise questions about current
policies and possibly antiquated practices, they create opportunities
to handle financial information with transparency and respectful
boundaries.

Sharing Information about Congregants

Often during pastoral visits in a home or the pastor's office, members share their life stories. Clergy learn personal information in these conversations that is sometimes quite intimate. How much of this information should clergy disclose? They have the obligation to guard this information with care. Congregants may feel betrayed if a clergyperson is inconsiderate about sensitive information and disrespectfully shares it with others. When a personal disclosure is passed to a third party without permission, trust is eroded. Unwittingly, clergy may break open a protected secret, unaware of the harm that can follow such disclosures. Disclosures can undermine the respect people have for one another, prematurely force a family to deal with a secret that they are not yet ready to process with other family members, and erode trust in the pastoral office. Clergy too frequently share things they should keep quiet about.

In every circumstance, with the exception of mandated reporting, clergy need to ask permission of a parishioner before sharing any information learned in the pastoral relationship. The always-ask-permission-to-share rule is especially relevant in domestic violence situations in which inappropriate disclosure can be lethal. Domestic violence prevention advocates emphasize that a clergyperson should absolutely never tell a batterer that his or her partner has talked about the abuse. Even a well-meaning confrontation in hopes of changing the batterer's behavior literally puts the victim's life at risk. The one exception to asking permission before disclosure is when someone has been abused or is at risk of harm; then the secret must be carefully and appropriately disclosed to legal authorities but not to other family members.

Knowing when to disclose information about a congregant may be challenging. What should a pastor do if a congregant who served time for molesting a child begins befriending a single church member with a daughter approximately the same age as the child the man had molested? A forward-thinking congregation would have already informed everyone of his background, but the young mother might have missed this crucial information. If the pastor shares the information directly with the mother, she might accuse the pastor of intervening in a perfectly decent relationship and possibly be inclined to defend the man and escalate their relationship. If the man tells the woman himself, he might spin the story and downplay the seriousness of the abuse. In this case, the pastor's best strategy would be to meet with the mother and the man at the pastor's office, with a lay leader present, and discuss the registered sex offender status and implications.

Sometimes a particularly problematic parishioner moves from one congregation to another. What do clergy from the first congregation tell the next congregation? Should someone warn the new clergyperson? If the congregant has a public record of the problematic behavior, the first clergyperson should release only what is already publicly accessible information without commentary or speculation. The information, shared in the most compassionate, appropriate, and limited manner necessary, protects the next congregation. The first clergyperson may also describe what process his or her congregation used to help a troublesome member or a registered sex offender maintain behavioral boundaries and the facts about the success or failure of such efforts.

If a registered sex offender leaves a congregation and joins a church down the street, his former pastor might decide to just let him go and hope that the new pastor checked all his new members through the online sex offender registry. A proactive pastor might want to be more certain that no one is at risk. The proactive pastor could take a printout of the Web site and a copy of his or her congregation's behavioral covenant to a meeting with the new pastor. Choosing words carefully, telling only what is necessary without emotional embellishment, the former pastor could disclose the information with respect and concern for the safety of members of the other congregation.

But what if the troubling behavior were stirring up conflict, degrading the leadership, or some other disruptive conduct? Some clergy might decide that former members are no longer any of their business. Some might decide that the congregant's new clergyperson wouldn't respond well to any comments, much less seemingly helpful information about new congregants. Each congregation is a different community. Each disclosure decision is unique.

Whenever a clear need to know exists on the part of the receiving congregation or clergy, the relevant information can be disclosed cautiously. A bishop may need to explain to a pastoral search committee that hiring a particular applicant would jeopardize the congregation's insurance coverage because of his history of sexual boundary violations. An executive presbyter may need to tell an executive presbyter in another state that the incoming pastor has had particular difficulties in his prior churches. When one congregant moves to another congregation, the first rabbi may feel her rabbinical colleague needs to know that when the congregant was president of her congregation there were many complaints and to be wary of his becoming a leader. Clergy, acting in good faith, may disclose information related to behaviors that put the congregation at risk, allegations of abuse, and public records of charges or complaints to those (and only those) who have a right and a need to know it—if each party has a common interest in the subject matter and if the information disclosed is factually accurate.

Sharing Information with Staff and Families

Clergy too often share information about parishioners with the office staff or with their families. This creates dilemmas for the staff member, spouse, and sometimes even the pastor's children. What do they then do with this information?

When more than one pastoral staff member is involved with the care of the congregation, what information is shared at staff meetings? A confidence shared with one staff member may not be intended for anyone else, even other staff. Each relationship is formed differently, and each person is entrusted with different information. In multiple-staff congregations, sometimes information is shared with the presumption that good pastoral care results when everyone on staff knows about a situation. However, damage can result when staff members haven't clarified with the parishioner what they will do with information received in a pastoral visit or a counseling appointment.

Parishioners presume that most disclosures to clergy are confidential, that is, known only to the two of them. For example, if a parishioner tells the pastor that she is a lesbian and can't tell anyone for fear of stigma, shame, and the loss of her job, the pastor must be very careful to respect that information boundary. Sharing information without permission to do so, even with others on staff, is a serious breach of trust. The congregation and any joining members need to know if clergy plan to share pastoral concerns with others. When too much clergy and staff disclosure is the norm, members may feel betrayed, disempowered, or victimized.

Guidelines can define what will be shared with others on the pastoral staff and with the full staff, including secretaries, volunteers, and others who have no direct responsibility for pastoral care. Congregations increase trust by creating and publishing interstaff communication guidelines, such as "Our front office staff will attempt to connect congregants directly to the senior pastor/rabbi/ designated staff for pastoral care. Leave personal and pastoral concerns directly on (name the individual)'s voice mail box, and they will be handled in a confidential manner." Guidelines help staff make decisions about the information they receive and keep it in the realm of limited access and only shared on a need-to-know basis.

A clergyperson who reveals too much to a spouse, due to habitually bad boundaries or perhaps in a dysfunctional response to overwork or burnout, reduces healthy functioning in her own family, as well as in her relationship to the congregation. If the clergyperson reveals to his spouse that a parishioner is having an affair, how will the spouse remain neutral in a conversation with that parishioner? If the rabbi tells her husband that a member of the congregation is trying to get her fired, how comfortably can the husband sit next to this man in worship? Clergy can learn to discuss their own issues in ministry without including others' names or details of situations, and thus enhance their spouse's or partner's ability to function in a more objective way in the congregation.

Clergy often need to process their thoughts and feelings about situations experienced in the congregation. More and more clergy rely on professional advice to help them sort through the information they have received and determine appropriate disclosure or confidentiality. Lawyers, therapists, psychologists, and consultants receive extensive training in what information should stay confidential information and what information must be legally and ethically reported to authorities, and they are good people to turn to when sorting through disclosure quandaries.

Like therapists, clergy can learn to protect the confidential nature of their trusted relationships and still process their thoughts and feelings, relieve stress, and engage in ethical ministry. With a trusted friend, partner, or colleague, clergy can talk about an issue without sharing details of the situation, the individuals involved, or details about the lives of those individuals. When clergy confide in someone, they can change the gender, the specific nature of the problem, and the identifying material in their story—as therapists do when sharing a client case in teaching, supervision, or even when receiving emotional support from their life partners.

In reality, very little personal information about congregants needs to be passed between present and succeeding clergy, between clergy and others on staff, and between clergy and spouses. When confidentiality is promised to congregants, their personal information must be protected, with the rare exception of disclosing information to avert danger to themselves or others. As information trustees, clergy must carefully choose when to be silent and when to speak. Too much disclosure by the clergy about their parishioners

creates other problems. Yet too little disclosure
atmosphere of secret keeping. Good self-care and
ss help clergy make wise decisions about how to
rmation; therefore they are less likely to be tempted
close or keep secrets—damaging relationships and con-
nal health.

Communicating about Registered Sex Offenders

The federal government instituted Megan's Law, which requires states to notify a community when a dangerous sexual predator moves into the area. Now, anyone can go online to learn where registered sex offenders of adults or children live across the country. Every state has different criteria for what offenses require registration and whose names appear on the National Sex Offender Registry, and the accuracy of the information available on the Web sites varies, but having access to such sensitive information has challenged congregations. The radical hospitality of the Jewish and Christian traditions encourages congregations to welcome all people into fellowship. The safety of both children and adults demands much more caution than an unquestioning, open invitation to participate in a faith community. How do congregations balance safety issues with hospitality to all?

Individuals trust their faith leaders to safeguard their well-being. They expect their leaders to reveal information about potential risks related to participation in their congregation. Along with assuming that insurance coverage for the congregation is adequate, members increasingly assume that their leaders screen volunteers working with children and notify parents of any of sex offenders who attend the congregation. Parents can monitor the National Sex Offender Registry themselves. However, clergy need to stay one step ahead of their congregants. When a parent discovers someone in the congregation on the list, hysteria and anger tend to escalate and clergy in particular get blamed for failure to protect the flock.

Someone on staff needs to regularly research this information and determine how can it be handled to both reduce the offender's shame and increase members' safety. Since not all sex offenders are at risk of repeating their crimes, not all situations should be handled in the same way. Some listings on the registry resulted from a single incident that occurred many years ago; some listings are recent or repeat offenses. Some offenders have not had treatment or taken treatment seriously, while others have worked hard at recovery and participated in programs to keep others and themselves from reoffending. Based on the offenses and the individual's efforts to make amends and heal, clergy and lay leaders have a broad range of options for disclosure of information on the registry. However, protecting this public information as if it were confidential or refusing to access it threatens the safety of others.

Three churches dealt differently with the public information on their state's online sex-offender list. Registered offenders were active in all three congregations, but leaders initially didn't know it. In one, the registered offender approached the minister and asked for her assistance in his recovery. Knowing that the counts against him were publicly accessible, he wanted to make sure the whole congregation knew his past, vigilantly supervised him, and supported him in his recovery.

In the second church, the minister had checked every member's zip code through the state's online sex offender registry and discovered no members listed. However, when he ran regular visitors' names, he discovered the best voice in the choir had served time for felony rape. Using that information, the minister met with the visitor, encouraged his continued participation in worship, but insisted that a covenant of boundaries be developed that would safeguard the church's participants and the visitor's own well-being.[1] The man signed the covenant, which promised he would always be escorted on church grounds and at any church-related events. He also agreed that not to date or socialize individually with any church members and to meet regularly with an accountability group. Layers of clear but compassionate disclosure followed—first to staff, then to the governing body, next to parents, and finally to the whole congregation.

The third pastor had refused to check the National Sex Offender Registry, but a mom in the congregation did, because one of the visitors gave her "the creeps." Earlier she had complained to the religious education staff about her concerns but was treated as if she were overreacting. So she turned to the Internet, and sure enough, the man's name was listed. If her earlier complaints seemed like overreacting, they were measured and calm compared to how furious and vocal she became. The man finally left the church during the uproar. His absence might have solved the problem, but still the mother finds it hard to trust anyone in the congregation to take her seriously or to protect her children.

When congregation leaders leave it up to a member to discover information that is publicly available, upset is bound to occur. The leaders appear irresponsible, naive, or secretive—rather than effective and trustworthy. Therefore leaders must determine whether anyone in the congregation or community is on the registry. Disclosing without malicious intent any names they find is vital for building trust and safety.

Communicating with Predecessor Clergy

When the United Methodist superintendent asked Ryan to go to a small community to serve as pastor, Ryan was surprised to learn that the preceding pastor, Stewart, was retiring and planning to stay in the neighborhood. In fact, the church hired him to stay on as church custodian. This both puzzled and upset Ryan, who worried that the former pastor would interfere with church growth and pastoral ministry. When someone died, whom would they call? When someone was irate about changes that Ryan was making, whom would they call?

A pastor who remains in any way connected to a congregation he or she used to serve can create a communication nightmare.

From the moment Pastor Ryan arrived at the church, Stewart had the advantage. After all, the old adage that knowledge is power rings true in congregations as well in other organizations. Stewart already had lines of communication with church members. He had intimate knowledge of church members—more than Ryan would have upon arrival, and perhaps more than Ryan would ever have. Depending on personalities and history, parishioners disclose differently to different pastors. A pastor who has performed a family funeral has a deeply intimate connection to that family at the time of loss and bereavement. This isn't likely to be replicated during the tenure of the next pastor, even if another family member were to die, because of differences in the time, place, and comfort in talking about the deceased or because of family dynamics.

The ideal situation is for clergy to move to another location when they leave a congregation. If clergy remain in the community, some denominations require that the individual worship at a different congregation for two years. In theory, that separation provides the newly arrived clergy with time to establish bonds without interference from the former clergy. However, even if Stewart had moved, communication with former congregants may continue. Members of Ryan's church might run certain leadership decisions by Stewart for his input. Or in a casual phone conversation, Stewart might offer an opinion about a program or another person. Limited-access information becomes more complicated when a retired pastor is secretly included in the loop.

If predecessor clergy continue a relationship with prior congregants (though ongoing relationships are discouraged), they must insist that conversations avoid subjects related to the leadership of the congregation. Predecessor clergy need to carefully redirect communication if gossip and rumor begin to swirl around current clergy or issues that are hotly debated within the congregation. Past clergy can act as dead-enders, rather than participate in the inappropriate discussions or become the source of previously privileged information. "Did you know that Mrs. Wilson passed away?" might be appropriate. However, "Did you know that Mrs.

Wilson refuses to donate ever since Ryan preached that sermon about forgiveness?" is out of bounds. If a former congregant wants to talk about the current state of the congregation or its current leadership, the former clergyperson needs to clearly redirect conversation to another topic.

Culturally based biases may influence whom congregants talk to. If asked to picture a leader in their minds, most people, depending on race and culture, still picture leaders who are middle-aged, Caucasian, tall, and male. Since men are more likely than women to be perceived as leaders, a gender stereotype could lead the congregation to continue to turn to and be influenced by the male former pastor, rather than the current female pastor. When a new clergyperson's first language differs from the dominant language in the worshiping community, people may avoid conversations due to the perception that they will not be understood or may not understand what is being said in response. When a new pastor's age, gender, or culture clash with congregants' expectations and comfort, congregants are more tempted to continue conversations with the previous pastor.

When new pastor Sharon learned of a church member's death, she called the bereaved widow, fully expecting to provide pastoral care and prepare for the service. "I'm so sorry about your husband," she said, "Can I drop by for a visit this afternoon?" The widow paused for a long while. "I'll make it brief," Sharon said, sensing that something was amiss. "Just a minute," she was told. "You can talk to my son." Her son said simply, "We're meeting with [retired] Pastor Eberson this afternoon; we've asked him to do the service."

Sharon bowed out gracefully but inwardly fumed about the situation. This would have been her first community appearance as the new pastor, an occasion when she would have gained the confidence of the congregation in her pastoral care and preaching ability. She asked Connie, the secretary, if she had heard anything about Pastor Eberson's involvement in the service or with the family. Connie noted that he had been there when the couple had a rocky marital episode and that he had counseled and married their son. "I can understand why they'd want him to do the service," Connie said. Sharon was emotionally conflicted. She understood the value of their long-term relationship and the intimate information that Eberson held about the family, but she felt that Pastor Eberson had undermined her ministry by not communicating with her and by agreeing to the service without her permission or participation. How would she ever gain the widow's trust and establish a caring relationship with her if parishioners continued to communicate with Pastor Eberson as if he were their pastor? She would always be the stepparent in the church family.

How can this problem be addressed? Predecessor clergy and clergy worshiping in congregations they do not serve need to be very clear that the authority of all pastoral functions and decisions rests with the current pastor or rabbi. If a retired pastor is invited to perform services, he or she should say to the parishioner, "I am honored that you are asking this of me. Your new pastor will handle that need well, and if she wants me to join her at your request, she can let me know how best to be included." Then members can be urged to talk with the current pastor or rabbi to decide how best to proceed. This approach clearly communicates to members who is in charge of services and other ministry during the current pastor's tenure. Most clergy welcome members of other denominations or faiths and former clergy in services of remembrance, weddings, and other rituals. But only at the invitation of the current pastor or rabbi can predecessor congregational leaders be comfortably included.

When clergy leave a parish, they sometimes feel as if the boundaries around private, confidential, and limited-access information are removed. They may meet with new staff and successors and divulge information from their experience or memories. This disclosure may provide a cathartic release for the exiting clergyperson but can have disastrous effects, leaving the new clergyperson with information he or she will have to deal with discretely. The disclosure may also violate the confidentiality or limited-access agreements of personnel committees and congregants. Finally, this sort of unloading of previously protected information can lead the new pastor to form premature opinions about congregants that perpetuate relational conflicts through generations of leadership.

In the counseling professions, a confidence remains intact for the life of the professional and any disclosure requires the written release of the client. If a psychologist counsels someone, he or she cannot acknowledge the relationship or any of the content of it even after the client dies. The ethical theory is that the client is always in a position of vulnerability and that the professional has the burden and privilege of being entrusted with this information. Clergy who retire or move from one congregation to another would do well to borrow from the ethical perspectives of other counseling professions. During a clergyperson's last days on the job, he or she can ask families receiving pastoral care for their permission to pass information about their needs to the incoming staff. Some will say yes and some will say no. When a yes is received, the next question is simply, "What would you like me to share with the new pastor about your situation?" This builds trust in the office of pastor or rabbi and provides a community where privacy is honored and respected.

Dealing with the Press

Mention of possible media attention terrifies most church leaders, although it should not. The press can actually be an ally in publicizing a congregation's response to tragedy. When one congregation found out that its former pastor had molested neighborhood children, the church held a press conference to express members' surprise, sorrow, and apologies to the victims and their families and also invited the whole community to a daylong training on protecting children from abuse. Local newspapers highlighted the story and the upcoming event; even the television station ran an outstanding feature about the congregation and its openness and commitment to safety of children in the community.

Another congregation with much less direct involvement with a child abuse situation refused to cooperate with press coverage. The abuse had occurred at a preschool that rented space from the church and was not affiliated at all with its ministry. Yet in ensuing months of press coverage, the church was named in every article. The reporter said she deliberately continued to refer to the church because the pastor had so adamantly refused to talk with her. The pastor missed an opportunity to offer a pastoral response to the community's pain and to highlight the value of the church's ministry.

The governing body of a third church argued into the night about whether to close a congregational meeting at which the pastor's arrest would be announced. Learning from the stories of two other churches, the leaders decided to welcome anyone who wished to attend the meeting. Instead of hiding in shame, the members exhibited how their faith lived, even through brokenness. One newspaper writer was so impressed that she actually joined the struggling congregation. Approaching media as allies in trying to disseminate the truth, instead of as enemies, gives congregational leaders a chance to tell their story rather than have it told for them.

Fear interferes with wise decisions about managing information. Never is this truer than when leaders are faced with potential lawsuits or when public attention is likely, especially from the media. Discernment is especially crucial when a complainant uses a threat to pressure congregational leaders into a specific response, such as a financial payoff. Statements such as "I will sue, if you don't . . ." or "I will tell the newspapers about this, if you don't . . ." should not influence leaders' decisions. The law protects individuals and congregations from extortion, yet the best protection is a clean record of astute information management, so that such a threat cannot be used as blackmail. Where there are no secrets (only information appropriately limited in its access), threat, extortion, and blackmail are ineffective. Congregational leaders can offer compassionate, well-bounded pastoral care when someone makes threats to sue, but they should refrain from being influenced by threats.

As in all information management decisions, being prepared can make the difference between effective communication and embarrassment. If a reporter phones with a question, a faith leader does not need to respond immediately and may want a cushion of time to take a deep breath and think through an answer. There is no such thing as "off the record," and leaders should be aware they are as likely to be misquoted as not. A polite response—"This is not a convenient time to talk right now; when may I call you back?"—provides the leader with some thinking space before jumping into a potentially public conversation.

Some basic questions should be considered when preparing a press release or congregational letter or getting ready for an interview.

- Who is the audience?
- What is the background of the audience members, and what do they know already and need to know now?
- What is their interest? How does this information affect them?
- What are their issues, concerns, and questions?
- How can the information help them?

The answers to these questions can help set the goals of the written or oral conversation, establish its key messages, and supply the necessary supporting facts.

Whether in a congregational meeting or a media interview, the audience receiving the information typically falls into three groups. Some will be supportive and encouraging. Others will be angry and will disagree or challenge almost anything said. The rest are undecided. The first group will believe what is said, but the second group will reject it, sometimes because of the content of the message or maybe because of who is speaking and what that person represents. The undecided should be the leaders' and communicators' target audience, because they will listen or read what is said. They can be influenced with a strong, positive message.

When speaking or writing, paying attention to "the three Cs"—clear, concise, and correct—improves the message.

Clear

- Tell the audience what they need to know and leave out everything else (especially emotional judgments, embellishments, or speculation), but don't forget anything important.
- Make sure your main point and preferred conclusion are apparent.
- Avoid jargon and acronyms.
- Consider how the audience is receiving your information. Remember that you almost never have people's complete attention.

Concise

- Use short, common words.
- Use personal pronouns (I, we, you, our, and so forth) and the active voice.
- Use short sentences.

Correct

- Be both grammatically and factually correct.
- Don't guess or speculate.
- When appropriate, say, "I don't know, but I'll find out for you" or "Here's who to ask that question."[2]

When releasing a public message, do the following:

- Think before you speak or write.
- Always make sure your facts are accurate.
- Remember your goals.
- Stress your positive central message(s) and supporting facts.
- Use concrete examples.
- Respect confidential and limited-access information.
- Remember the best answer to an either-or question is often neither, but something different or another question.
- Remember that nothing is "off the record."
- Recap your central message(s) before you finish.

In a congregation that decided to hold a holy union service for a gay couple, a member of the congregation who was against it phoned the local newspaper and radio stations. He then told the pastor, "If you go ahead with that service, I'll have the media and community all coming to witness it." The pastor met with key lay leaders, and they decided that the publicity would be handled carefully. They didn't want anyone who didn't know the couple to crash the ceremony, so they set up a pressroom. Leaders notified the media themselves and invited reporters to come to the church library during the ceremony for coffee and doughnuts. If reporters wished to make a story of the event, the pastor would be available after the service to be interviewed. The congregation's proactive stance resulted in silencing the media, and the service was held without disruption. The leftover doughnuts were enjoyed by board members who had posted themselves outside the church to redirect uninvited guests and the media to the library.

Having painful congregational incidents publicized might seem frightening, but publicity can also be used to a congregation's advantage. Regardless of how horrible the information is that may be revealed to the public, the attitude and approach of congregational leaders can create as sense of calm and clarity, rather than panic or anxiety.

Challenge or Opportunity?

The situations reviewed here call for the creation of, or review of, policies and procedures regarding sharing information. Though challenging at first, such a policy creation and review provides the opportunity for increasing trust among leaders and members of the congregation. Trusted leaders highly honor the information they are given. They don't repeat stories without permission unless mandated to file protective reports. They don't use information about donors to take advantage of them or to embarrass them. They don't pass on old stories as if former protections on communication had expired and they can now expose former intimacies. Instead, they ask, "What would you like me to tell others about this?" They describe to whom and why they must pass on information when necessary. They honor confidentiality, teach others to understand limited access, and build communities where trust is high and interpersonal safety is ensured.

Chapter 12

Speaking the Truth in Love

The century-old church, Hampshire Hills, had surrounded itself with a stately wrought-iron fence to keep children from riding their bikes through their peaceful memorial gardens and throwing rocks at the classic stained glass windows. A homeless man from the nearby downtown had parked his grocery cart in the carefully pruned bushes. The building itself stood high above town, its granite block exterior making it a fortress as well as a center for worship.

The congregation preferred a traditional service in its impressive, beamed sanctuary. Members gathered afterwards in a modern, beautifully painted fellowship hall, where even the notes on the bulletin boards were arranged as if by an artist. Young and old lined up single file for the coffee, and cups of apple juice were passed to youngsters over the kitchen counter. Most people sat at tables to linger over their cookies and were conscientious about keeping the hall spotless. However, the buzz of conversation stopped abruptly when a young man leaped up on a table, shouting that he wanted everyone's attention. No one can remember exactly what he said, but many recall being terrified by his rage and confused by his words—something about being molested by a prior pastor and the congregation covering it up. He said he intended to "take down" the church by revealing all its secrets. The senior pastor stared in disbelief until a parishioner shoved him forward saying, "Do something!"

As he moved forward to talk to the young man, the scripture passage, "Nothing is covered up that will not be uncovered," (Luke 12:2) haunted him. Though it would take the pastor a while to discover all of the hidden stories, he knew it had taken many silent witnesses and many years of cover-ups to result in such a rage-filled disruption. That Sunday morning revealed that the congregation had been mismanaging information for years.

Withheld information intensifies as if corked until it explodes, while often in the same congregation gossip and rumors whirl around without containment. "Congregations release information they should hold on to—and hold on to information they should release," one minister complained. Rather than discerning the appropriate time to be silent and time to speak (Eccles. 3:7), too many congregations practice *impression* management rather than *information* management.

Congregations tend to casually spread personal information about parishioners, yet guard institutional information that might damage the reputation of the church, even if that information seems crucial to the health and healing of the congregation. Faith leaders can be tempted to maintain an illusion rather than seeing and telling the truth and promoting transparency. Hampshire Hills certainly managed to look good but at a serious cost to members' integrity, trust, and spiritual well-being. Congregations sometimes look healthy, but in reality beneath that image, they may have problems they cannot identify.

"Almost every time we at the Alban Institute are asked to help a congregation, people will tell us that the problem is 'communication,'" Loren Mead once wrote.[1] Congregations complain that people do not seem to know the information they need, information is misinterpreted, rumors and gossip flourish, or private material has been leaked publicly. Often congregants hear sensitive information that they have no need or right to know, yet they lack the information they do need to make reasonable decisions at a congregational meeting. The informal, and sometimes unhelpful, nature of congregational communication management leads to frequent joking about church business being done in the parking lot rather than at official meetings or about the speed with which congregational rumors fly through the phone lines.

In this resource we have described the dangers of denial, deception, and ignorance. Congregants and leaders may have the wrong information, may be intentionally misled by another, or may lack the information that would reveal the reality of a situation. Ignorance, or simply not having access to necessary information, may be more innocent than intentional deception, yet the result may potentially be as harmful, especially if the ignorance comes from secret keeping.

To create healthier congregational systems, both clergy and congregational leaders need to acknowledge the damage their communication patterns have created in the past and correct them in the present congregational culture. How would the people of Hampshire Hills go about doing that? How will the current pastor deal with the deception of the past? The task at hand is to reduce shame about past behavior while establishing a plan for change.

The Clergy Role

Clergy have a key role in creating healthy congregational systems. The new pastor of Hampshire Hills has quite a task ahead in creating transparency and restoring people's trust. While one pastor cannot by himself or herself redress years of clergy scandals and negative history, he or she can name the damage of misconduct and then help the congregation become aware of the way its communication patterns may have played a part in it.

Clergy of every faith tradition have the authority and power to control the dissemination of information. Unfortunately, they have not always acted in the best interests of the congregation as a whole and have harmed others with both silence and disclosure. John Wesley used the power of his office to shame and excommunicate a woman he was in love with. After having broken away from the

Catholic Church in protest against abuses of power, Martin Luther ironically asserted the right of his new church to use deception. "Luther defended 'a good hearty lie for the sake of the good and for the Christian Church, a lie in case of necessity, a useful lie.' Such lies, he said, 'would not be against God.'"[2] Clergy are too often tempted to protect the institution or themselves rather than the individuals within them. Lacking integrity in the management and use of personal information, clergy in all faith traditions have brought more harm than protection to the very institutions they have served.

Clergy who confess and name realities within the congregation give permission for individuals to tell the truth as well. Clergy who dare to ask the hard questions about the life of the congregation find places of darkness that still need healing. Each congregation has a history that is more about the people than the date of the groundbreaking. Clergy who identify negative communication behavior and teach new ways to manage congregational information can help transform their faith community.

Often a congregation blames one individual clergyperson for poor communication boundaries and other boundary crossings, while the problems continue from one generation to the next. Or they eagerly seek a new rabbi or pastor who can work a miracle and change the congregation—without changing a single individual within it! So, to begin changing a congregation's communication culture, clergy need to be personally rigorous and ethical in their communications and behavior and develop support and accountability systems. Every clergyperson needs to meet monthly with a professional supervisor to review interpersonal or systemic issues in his or her ministry. This supervisor could be a spiritual director; a credentialed therapist; a congregational consultant; or someone else with professional training, insight, and the ability give honest and constructive feedback.

Supervision can help clergy directly address areas where personal and professional issues converge. Clergy, like all people, tend to repeat patterns they learned in their family of origin. For example, those who were raised with family secrets tend to handle secret-keeping situations as they would have in their childhood homes. With growth and supervision, however, the clergyperson can learn to avoid the pitfalls of communication that impair individual and congregational functioning. Supervision can also help clergy clean up the congregational communication patterns that have injured them, rather than taking those patterns personally. A good deal of courage is needed for clergy to name and correct poor communication. Supervision provides an arena in which clergy can discuss the keeping or disclosing of confidences. Supervision can help clergy honor the power of each communication.

The Role of Lay Leaders

Clergy who name and stop negative communication behavior can help reshape congregational culture. They cannot do this alone, however. As lay leaders join the work of communication transformation, the number of individuals modeling more effective communication increases, as does the possibility of changing old patterns. For example, it took clergy and lay leaders in a united effort to correct a communication situation at First Church Morgantown that had way gotten out of hand. When upset with the sermon or worship experience, most people simply complained about it in the community. They told their mechanic or their hairdresser or the children's teacher at school. They simply refused to talk to the people in charge of worship or to the pastor, because, they said, "It wouldn't make any difference; the committee is just made up of the pastor's friends anyway." Whether or not that was true, that reason was used to justify their negative behavior. They became a congregation of habitual whiners, a place where everyone felt disempowered. Even though the president of the congregation knew how to correct the situation, he felt helpless and hopeless to implement his knowledge.

Whole congregations can identify themselves as victims of something or someone. The blame may be placed on current or past clergy or laity. Sometimes the blame is placed on a bishop or a superintendent or the polity of the congregation. "Victim" congregations create a place where individuals feel victimized and actually do become victims. This sense of powerlessness is debilitating—and yet it can be changed.

Lay leaders need to *believe* that change is possible, that the congregation and individual leaders and clergy are not powerless. In fact, people within a congregation have the power to change it. It took only one board member saying, "Please stop spreading negativity about the congregation and come talk to us at a meeting," and the congregational culture at First Church Morgantown began to change. The board worked eagerly with a consultant it hired and reviewed communication practices throughout the congregation. Later when board members shaped protective policies regarding ministerial ethics, personnel, sexual harassment and abuse prevention, and safe sanctuary, they developed documents that described appropriate communication channels for their faith community.

At another church, after years of negative gossip and patterns of irresponsible communication, three lay leaders met with their new pastor and asked her to work with them for healing. They began their conversation much like a 12-step group meeting—by saying they knew that they were powerless over the blaming, backbiting, rumormongering, and triangulation that was going on in the congregation. They also knew that with God's help they could begin a process that would change the congregation. Despite the reputation of the congregation and its history of criticism toward clergy, the new pastor was moved by their courage and full disclosure and agreed to work with them in healing the congregation.

Where did they begin? They set ground rules for talking to each other and about each other, rules that were later adopted by the governing council. With more and more members of the congregation, they began to share their own wounds, hurts that had resulted from the culture of negativity within the congregation. They set up forums in which individuals could safely talk about their relationships with one another and the way they had betrayed each other with hurtful words. Eventually, others in the congregation realized they too had participated in the problems by making decisions without listening to various opinions and controlling others by keeping secrets. It all began with just three lay leaders who changed the whole congregation by confessing their own part in letting bad behaviors continue, wounding people with gossip and innuendo. Three people seeking justice and healing turned the congregation around. In less than a year they had boosted attendance; supported their new pastor; removed leaders from office who would not comply with appropriate guidelines for disclosure; and set the course for ongoing growth in faith, financial strength, and worship attendance.

Clergy and Laity Working Together

Unhealthy communication patterns create a culture where deception is possible, where blame replaces responsibility, and where power distortions bring growth to a slow and steady halt. In congregations like Hampton Hills, where a person apparently misused his power, three patterns of poor informational boundaries are usually evident: (1) information is censored to hide the abuse, (2) confidential material is leaked by the person abusing power, and (3) communication breaks down among congregants. Crucial information is concealed and private information is revealed. In incidents of sexual boundary crossings, it is likely that communication and information boundaries have also been crossed. In fact, a lack of communication boundaries can be a signpost that other boundaries of appropriate behavior may be ignored. That is why it is crucial to address communication issues as soon as negative patterns arise. When communication boundaries are sound, other types of boundaries are less likely to be violated.

Local congregational disclosure problems are established within the culture at large. Determining what information should be shared or protected is especially difficult in a culture where disclosure is highly valued, in which individuals are encouraged to be open and forthright with their friends and therapists—all the while proclaiming the right to privacy. People share intimate details about their private lives in books and on tell-all television programs but complain about the amount of data the government and companies collect on them. In such a paradoxically private-but-open culture, how can a congregation exercise faith-based discernment to balance the need for the majority of its information to be open with the need to protect certain disclosures? Appropriate confidentiality protects the integrity and dignity of an individual worshiper. Prudent limited-access information protects disclosures within committees while they process difficult personnel problems. All the while, transparency enhances community trust and communication.

As clergy and lay leaders become conscious of the damage caused by negative communication patterns, they can open a wide arena for congregational discussion about *how* the congregation communicates: the protection of privacy, community communication patterns, and communication challenges in congregational life. Leaders also can encourage discussion of *what* the congregation talks about. During an open forum, the following sample questions invite conversation:

- What would you least want a newcomer to find out about your congregation?
- Do parts of your congregation's history cause you embarrassment?
- Has the congregation been carrying secrets of some kind?
- Are there people in the history of the congregation who are never mentioned?
- Are there procedures that you don't talk about?
- Are certain topics avoided because they make people uncomfortable?
- Have there been any accusations of sexual boundary crossings here?

- Is the congregation grieving losses, such as a beloved pastor, decline in attendance and membership, or the death of a prominent leader?
- What subjects cannot be openly discussed?[3]

If a congregation is harboring major secrets, such questions could create turmoil temporarily, even when communication guidelines are honored. As people share their personal experiences and feelings and are heard without judgment, they can slowly heal. Injustices can be addressed, amends made, and the path laid for courageous, enduring transparency.

It Starts with Each of Us

When people "walk the talk," they have faith-life integrity. When people "talk the walk," the intention behind their communication matches the precepts of their faith. Choices about when to speak and when to remain silent are never neutral. Sharing information can be well intentioned—or deceptive. Withholding information can be well intentioned—or deceptive. Every choice we make about communication stems from some conscious or unconscious expected outcome, which may be helpful or harmful to the health of the congregation. To create transparent congregations, each leader needs to "talk" a walk that is consistent with his or her faith.

Communication choices cannot be separated from faith. Religious leaders' complicity in illusionary thinking, deceitfulness, secrecy, and ignorance shapes a congregation's theology. And in turn, some theologies encourage giving false assurance, keeping secrets about the community's dysfunction, and disguising reality. When truth is obfuscated or mismanaged, we must ask ourselves if our God is one of good impressions and "niceness"—or one of truth and justice. If our communication creates a "workable fantasy" rather than transparent community, Old Testament scholar Walter

Brueggemann warns, "Such fantasy will bring devastation upon a deceived community."[4]

Our congregations should be as transparent as our faith, because revelation is the essence of Christianity. Ethicist James Gaffney urges to his own Catholic Church towards transparency, arguing:

> We do not have a Church because we believe in God. We have a Church because we believe in a revealing God. And the measure of the Church's authenticity and fidelity is, above all, its service of God precisely as revealing. There is a more than verbal irony in the idea of a concealing Church rendering service to a revealing God. . . . Candor and openness are signs of the Church's health; secretiveness is a symptom of its ailments or a side effect of attempts to cure them.[5]

The candor and openness of transparent congregations require sharing truthfully all that should be known and require, as well, the wisdom to know that not everything that could be said should be said. With courage and discernment, faith leaders can talk their faith walk as they address old wounds and build up the community in a spirit of integrity and love. The truth about God and the truth about the world are intimately connected; we must tell them both.

Appendix

Who Has the Right to
Know What Information

The chart on the following pages shows individuals and groups of people who have a right to certain information about a congregation at that level.

WHO	WHAT
Public	A congregation's incorporation information
Public	Denominational polity and governance
Public	A congregation's denominational affiliation
Public	Names of clergy presently serving the congregation
National/international judicatory	A congregation's policies, guidelines, standards, code of ethics
National/international judicatory	The number of members in its congregations
National/international judicatory	Names of elected officers in its congregations
National/international judicatory	Financial information
National/international judicatory	Movement of clergy from one congregation to another
Local judicatory	Major internal conflicts within the congregation
Local judicatory	Encumbrance of property
Local judicatory	How membership numbers are determined in that congregation
Local judicatory	Worship attendance figures
Congregational members	Roles and responsibilities of pastors, staff, and volunteers
Congregational members	Individual staff salaries, in most denominations
Congregational members	Details of contracts and job descriptions
Congregational members	Details of insurance coverage
Congregational members	Budget and benevolences

Congregational members	Contents of minutes of the congregation's governing body
Congregational members	Matters related to the electing or selecting of lay leaders
Congregational members	Matters related to the calling of their clergy
Congregational members	Some matters related to the pastoral relationship
Congregational members	Matters related to buying, mortgaging, or selling real property
Congregational members	Names of other members
Congregation's governing body	Basic reasons for staff departures or changes
Congregation's governing body	Basic reasons for volunteer departures or changes
Congregation's governing body	Information about particular congregational problems
Congregation's governing body	Pledging amounts and patterns
Subcommittee of governing body	Personnel evaluations
Subcommittee of governing body	Goals for probationary employees
Subcommittee of governing body	Employment problems
Subcommittee of governing body	Results of screening of staff and volunteers (references, fingerprinting, and the like)
Subcommittee of governing body	Reasons for staff departures
Subcommittee of governing body	Reasons for volunteer departures
Subcommittee of governing body	Donor records
Clergy	All the information above

Notes

Chapter 1

1. Kibbie Simmons Ruth, "A Decision-Making Process for Managing Sensitive Information in Congregations of the San Francisco Presbytery" (Doctor of Ministry thesis, Pacific School of Religion, Berkeley, CA, 2002).

Chapter 2

1. Paul Tournier, *Secrets,* trans. M. E. Bratcher (Richmond, VA: John Knox Press, 1963).

2. Sissela Bok, *Secrets: On the Ethics of Concealment and Revelation* (New York: Vintage Press, 1989), 5-6.

3. Evan Imber-Black, *The Secret Life of Families* (New York: Bantam Publishing, 1998), 4.

Chapter 3

1. Edwin H. Friedman, *Generation to Generation: Family Process in Church and Synagogue* (New York: Guilford, 1985), 52.

2. Ibid.

3. Erving Goffman, *Stigma: Notes on the Management of Spoiled Identity* (New York: Simon and Schuster, 1963), 42.

4. Kenneth R. Mitchell, *Multiple Staff Ministries* (Philadelphia: Westminster/John Knox Press, 1988), 130.

Chapter 4

1. Gordon Willard Allport and Leo Postman, *The Psychology of Rumor* (New York: Russell and Russell, Inc., 1965), ix.

2. Ralph L. Rosnow and Gary Alan Fine, *Rumor and Gossip: The Social Psychology of Hearsay* (New York: Elsevier Scientific Publishing Co., 1976), 51

3. Allport and Postman, *Psychology of Rumor*, 198.

4. Ibid., 167.

5. Hal Morgan and Kerry Tucker, *Rumor!* (New York: Penguin Books, 1984), 19.

6. Rosnow and Fine, *Rumor and Gossip*, 41.

7. Allport and Postman, *Psychology of Rumor*, 46.

8. Rosnow and Fine, *Rumor and Gossip*, 74.

9. Allport and Postman, *Psychology of Rumor*, 170.

10. Rosnow and Fine, *Rumor and Gossip*, 13.

11. Kathleen Fearn-Banks, *Crisis Communications: A Casebook Approach* (Mahwah, NJ: Lawrence Erlbaum Associates, Publishers, 2002), 44.

12. Allport and Postman, *Psychology of Rumor*, 33.

13. Ibid., 169.

14. See www.loc.gov/folklife/guides/rumors.html.

15. William L. White, *The Incestuous Workplace: Stress and Distress in the Organizational Family* (Center City, MN: Hazelden, 1997), 73.

16. R. I. M. Dunbar, "Co-Evolution of Neocortex Size, Group Size and Language in Humans," *Behavioral and Brain Sciences* 16(4): 681.

17. Nigel Nicholson, "The New Word on Gossip," *Psychology Today* (May/June 2001), http://psychologytoday.com/articles/pto-20010501-000022.html (accessed May 9, 2007).

18. Deborah Tannen, *You Just Don't Understand: Women and Men in Conversation* (New York: Ballantine Books, 1990), 107.

19. William H. Willimon, "Heard About the Pastor Who ... ? Gossip as an Ethical Activity," *Christian Century* 107 (October 31, 1990): 995.

Chapter 6

1. Karen McClintock, *Preventing Sexual Abuse in Congregations* (Herndon, VA: Alban Institute, 2004), 138.

2. Wendell E. Miller, "True Love Deals with Problems," *Biblical Counseling Association,* 1988, http://www.biblical-counsel.org/qa-26.htm (accessed January 3, 2007).

3. American Association of Pastoral Counselors, Code of Ethics (Amended April 28, 1994), "Principle IV-Confidentiality," D, http://www.aapc.org/ethics.cfm (accessed May 10, 2007). American Psychological Association, Ethical Principles of Psychologists and Code of Conduct (Effective June 1, 2003), "Privacy and Confidentiality: Disclosures," 4.05b, http://www.apa.org/ethics/code2002.html (accessed May 10, 2007).

4. American Psychological Association, Ethical Principles of Psychologists and Code of Conduct (Effective June 1, 2003), "Privacy and Confidentiality: Consultations," 4.06, http://www.apa.org/ethics/code2002.html (accessed May 10, 2007).

5. Kim Lawton, "Interview: Nancy Ammerman," *Religion and Ethics Newsweekly* Episode 535 (May 3, 2002), http://www.pbs.org/wnet/religionandethics/week535/nammerman.html (accessed January 25, 2007).

Chapter 7

1. Julia Day (lawyer, Atlantic Insurance, San Carlos, CA) interview with Kibbie Ruth, August 26, 1998. According to Day, juror bias is particularly evident in cases involving more conservative churches such as the Jubilee Christian Church, which she represented when it was sued for not protecting young boys from its abusive pastors (settled out of court, August 1998). Impartial legal decisions are particularly difficult when

a case involves a faith group, because jurors often have biases related to beliefs and the institutions that promote them.

2. *Lemon v. Kurtzman*, 403 U.S. 602 (1971), establishing what is legally known as the Lemon Test, further clarified in *Wolman v. Walter*, 433 U.S. 229, 236 (1977).

3. *Eugene Eliason v. The Church of Jesus Christ of Latter Day Saints* (1984), in Mark A. Taylor, "Sin and Death in Mormon Country: A Latter-day Tragedy," available from http://www.solotouch.com/res.php?t=a&num=22 (accessed May 5, 2007).]

4. *First Covenant Church v. City of Seattle*, 120 Wn.2d 203, 218 (1992), citing Sherbert v. Verner, 374 U.S. 398 (1963).

5. *Madsen v. Erwin*, 395 Mass. 715, 481 N.E.2d 1160, 1167 (1985).

6. *Watson v. Jones* 80 U.S. 679, 722 (1871).

7. Arthur Gross Schaefer, "Divine Immunity: Should Clergy Be Subject to a Standard of Care?" *CPCU (Chartered Property and Casualty Underwriters) Journal* 40, no. 4 (December 1987): 218. Insurance companies now settle many cases out of court to avoid expensive legal defense fees, whether or not the clergyperson was at fault.

8. John C. Bush and William Harold Tiemann, *The Right to Silence: Privileged Clergy Communication and the Law* (Nashville, TN: Abingdon Press, 1989), 201.

9. Schaefer, "Divine Immunity," 217.

10. *Nally v. Grace Community Church of the Valley* 47 Cal. 3d 278, 253 Cal. Rptr. 97, 763 P.2d 948 (1988).

11. John F. Wagner Jr., "Cause of Action for Clergy Malpractice: Background and Summary," *American Law Reports* ALR4th, October 2006. See also Mark A. Weitz, *Clergy Malpractice in America: Nally v. Grace Community Church of the Valley* (Lawrence, KS: University Press of Kansas, 2001).

12. Richard R. Hammar, *Church Law and Tax Report* 12, no. 4 (July/ August 1998): 26.

13. Efforts to use "breach of fiduciary duty" include U.S.C.A. Const. Amend. 1. *F.G. v. MacDonnell*, 150 N.J. 550, 696 A.2d 697 (1997), *Teadt v. Lutheran Church Missouri Synod*, 237 Mich. App. 567, 603 N.W.2d

816 (1999), *Wende C. v. United Methodist Church*, 776 N.Y.S.2d 390 (App. Div. 4th Dept. 2004), *U.S. C.A. Const. Amend. 1. Langford v. Roman Catholic Diocese of Brooklyn*, 177 Misc. 2d 897, 677 N.Y.S.2d 436 (Sup. Ct. 1998).

14. *F.G. v. MacDonnell*, 696 A.2d 697 (N.J. 1997) in which a woman alleged that her Episcopal priest improperly induced her to engage in a sexual relationship while acting as her pastoral counselor. She claimed his conduct caused her physical and psychological injury and economic loss, and because his alleged wrongdoing fell outside Episcopal doctrine, the First Amendment should not protect him.

15. Lindell L. Gumper, *Legal Issues in the Practice of Ministry* (Birmingham, MI: Psychological Studies, 1981), 23. See also the RESTATEMENT (SECOND) OF TORTS § 596 (1977), 15.

16. McKinney's CPLR 4505. *Lightman v. Flaum*, 97 N.Y.2d 128, 736 N.Y.S.2d 300, 761 N.E.2d 1027 (2001). For more information about why "every American court to consider the issue has refused to adjudicate claims of clergy malpractice," see article and footnote no. 7 of http://www.churchstatelaw.com/commentaries/WatsonvJones.asp (accessed April 13, 2007).

17. *Hester v. Barnett* 723 S.W.2d 544 (Mo.App.1987).

18. *Doe v. Oregon Conference of Seventh-Day Adventists*, 199 Or. App. 319, 111 P.3d 391 (2005).

19. American Law Institute, RESTATEMENT (SECOND) OF TORTS § 559 (1977).

20. George P. Rice, "Defamation by Slander," in *Law for the Public Speaker* (Boston: The Christopher Publishing House, 1958), 114.

21. BLACK'S LAW DICTIONARY 505, rev. 4th ed. (St. Paul: West Publishing, 1968).

22. Rice, "Defamation by Slander," 115.

23. Sally A. Johnson, "Legal Issues in Clergy Sexual Boundary Violation Matters," in *Boundary Wars: Intimacy and Distance in Healing Relationships*, ed. Katherine Hancock Ragsdale (Cleveland: Pilgrim Press, 1996), 172.

24. *Davis v. Black*, 70 Ohio App. 3d 359, 591 N.E.2d 11 (1991), in which a discharged church secretary brought claims for (1) sexual

harassment against a pastor, (2) retaliatory discharge against the church arising from the sexual harassment complaint, and (3) intentional infliction of emotional distress and defamation against the church and the pastor.

25. *Murphy v. Harety*, 238 Or. 228, 393 P.2d 206 (1964).

26. Cynthia S. Mazur and Ronald K. Bullis, *Legal Guide for Day-to-Day Church Matters: A Handbook for Pastors and Church Members* (Cleveland: United Church Press, 1994), 53.

27. Thomas F. Taylor, "Will Your Church Be Sued? How to Anticipate and Avoid Lawsuits in an Age of Litigation Overkill," *Christianity Today* 41, no. 1 (January 6, 1997): 46.

28. Ronald K. Bullis and Cynthia S. Mazur, "Church Liability for Staff Conduct," *The Christian Ministry* 27 (March-April 1996): 15-18.

29. *Funkhouser v. Wilson*, 950 P.2d 501 (Wash. App. 1998).

30. Lynn R. Buzzard and Thomas S. Brandon Jr., *Church Discipline and the Courts* (Wheaton, IL: Tyndale House Publishers, Inc., 1987), 270.

31. Justice Joseph Story, *Commentaries on the Constitution of the United States*, quoted in Buzzard and Brandon, 147.

32. According to the RESTATEMENT OF TORTS 2d § 652A (1977), the four distinct forms of invasion of privacy are: (1) the unreasonable intrusion upon the seclusion of another; (2) the appropriation of another's name or likeness; (3) the unreasonable publicity given to another's private life; and (4) publicity that unreasonably places another in a false light before the public.

33. William L. Prosser, "Privacy," *California Law Review* 48 (1960): 383-389.

34. An example of "false light" invasion of privacy is the minister who from the pulpit praised a parishioner recovering from a past life of prostitution that no one else had known about prior to the minister's comments. The parishioner had not wanted others to know.

35. Rodney A. Smolla, "Privacy and Related Torts," in *Smolla and Nimmer on Freedom of Speech* (New York: Clark Boardman Callaghan, 1997), § 24:5.

36. Richard R. Hammar, ed., *Legal Reference Library, 1998 Edition.* CD-ROM (Matthews, NC: Christian Ministry Resources, 1998, § 704). The facts may be true but have the effect of attributing to the person attitudes or actions that are not accurate or at least are no longer accurate. "[A] reasonable person would feel justified in feeling seriously aggrieved by its dissemination."

37. Buzzard and Brandon, *Church Discipline and the Courts*, 114.

38. Ibid.

39. *Gunn v. Mariners Church*, 2005 WL 1253953 (Cal. App. 2005, unpublished).

40. *Guinn v. Church of Christ of Collinsville*, 775 P.2d 766 (Oakla. 1989).

41. *St. Luke Evangelical Lutheran Church, Inc. v. Smith*, 74 Md.App., 353 537 A.2d 1196 (1988).

42. The Book of Discipline of the United Methodist Church, 2004, ¶ 341.5 (Nashville: The United Methodist Publishing House, 2004).

43. Buzzard and Brandon, *Church Discipline and the Courts*, 127.

44. A thorough review of the differing state statutes regarding the clergy-penitent can be seen in "Addressing the Tension Between the Clergy-Communicant Privilege and the Duty to Report Child Abuse in State Statutes" by Norman Abrams and can be viewed online at http://www.bc.edu/schools/law/lawreviews/meta-elements/journals/bclawr/44_4/08_FMS.htm (accessed April 13, 2007).

45. Presbyterian Church-USA, 185th General Assembly Background Paper, "Illustrations of Invasions of Privacy And Its Control," *Church and Society* (November-December 1974), 37.

46. United Press International, August 7, 1985, PM cycle.

47. The Book of Discipline of the United Methodist Church, 2004, ¶ 341.5 (Nashville: The United Methodist Publishing House, 2004).

48. As of 2005, 25 states required clergy to report abuse, and 18 others required everyone to report abuse, thereby including clergy and congregational lay staff and volunteers.

49. Specific information can be found at the federal Web site "Child Welfare Information Gateway," http://www.childwelfare.gov/

systemwide/laws_policies/statutes/clergymandated.cfm (accessed April 13, 2007).

50. *Alexander v. Culp*, 705 N.E.2d 378 (Ohio App. 8th Dist. 1997).

51. *Lightman v. Flaum* 736 N.Y.S.2d 300 (2001). In that case a wife confided in two separate rabbis concerning her infidelity, and both rabbis disclosed the confidences to the husband and went as far as to submit affidavits attesting to the information in the parties' divorce proceeding.

Chapter 8

1. "Principles are self-evident, self-validating natural laws . . . [that] apply all the time in all places . . . [and] unlike values, are objective and external." Stephen R. Covey, *Principle-Centered Leadership* (New York: Summit Books, 1990), 19. Fairness, equity, justice, integrity, honesty, and trust are examples of principles.

2. See William L. White, *The Incestuous Workplace: Stress and Distress in the Organizational Family* (Center City, MN: Hazelden, 1997) for an excellent discussion on destructive systems.

Chapter 9

1. Craig T. Palmer, "When to Bear False Witness: An Evolutionary Approach to the Social Context of Honesty and Deceit Among Commercial Fishers," *Zygon: Journal of Religion and Science* 28, no. 4 (December 1993): 455.

Chapter 10

1. Liberally adapted from Karpman's basic concepts as described in S. B. Karpman "Fairy Tales and Script Drama Analysis," *Transactional Analysis Bulletin* 7 (April 1968): 26.

2. Ralph L. Rosnow and Gary Alan Fine, *Rumor and Gossip: The Social Psychology of Hearsay* (New York: Elsevier Scientific Publishing Co., 1976), 121.

3. William H. Willimon, "Heard About the Pastor Who . . . ? Gossip as an Ethical Activity" *Christian Century* (October 31, 1990): 996.

Chapter 11

1. See resources at www.kyros.org for a sample covenant with an offender in a congregation.

2. Adapted from Kathi McDonald and Michael Sampson, "When 60 Minutes Wants a Word With You," (St. Louis, MO, 1998).

Chapter 12

1. Loren B. Mead, *More Than Numbers: The Ways Churches Grow* (Herndon, VA: Alban Institute, 1993), 77.

2. Allen Verhey, "Directions: Is Lying Always Wrong?" *Christianity Today* 43, no. 24 (May 1999): 68.

3. Adapted from Kenneth R. Mitchell, *Multiple Staff Ministries* (Philadelphia: Westminster/John Knox Press, 1988), 71-72.

4. Walter Brueggemann, "Truth-Telling as Subversive Obedience," *Journal for Preachers* 20 (Lent 1997): 4.

5. James Gaffney, "Access to Information," *A Catholic Bill of Rights* (Kansas City, MO: Sheed & Ward, 1988), 43.